SERVICE BADGES AND EMBLEMS: 1

THIRD REICH CLOTH INSIGNIA

Ian Allan
PUBLISHING

The large size Luftwaffe national
emblem as worn on an officer's
cloak. Displayed on the area covering
the wearer's left upper arm, thus
positioning the eagle to face the front,
this emblem was worked in silver
bullion threads for officers and in gold
bullion for general officers.

SERVICE BADGES AND EMBLEMS: 1

THIRD REICH CLOTH INSIGNIA

Brian L. Davis and
Ian Westwell

First published 2003

ISBN 0 7110 2930 X

Published by Ian Allan Publishing

an imprint of Ian Allan Publishing Ltd, Hersham, Surrey, KT12 4RG

Printed and bound in the United Arab Emirates.

British Library Cataloguing in Publication Data
A CIP catalogue record for this book is available from the British Library

NOTES
1. Editorially it is the usual practice to put into italics all words that are not in English. Because of the number of German words this approach has not been adopted in this book.

2. Wherever possible translations of German words are given in brackets or in the Glossary on page 188.

3. All photographs are either taken by the author or from his collection.

RIGHT: **Pre-1935 SA-Reserve armband. See page 95.**

FAR RIGHT: **A member of the German Marineartillerie standing guard duty at a shore base somewhere in the Mediterranean theatre.**

Contents

Introduction

This volume provides a history of the cloth badges worn by members of the various organisations that were at the heart of the Nazi Party and the Third Reich, and covers a period from the end of World War I to the Allied victory over Germany in 1945. It particularly concentrates on the years from Hitler's assumption of power as chancellor in January 1933 to the conclusion of World War II and the destruction of the Hitler state – an era that saw a vast expansion in the range of Nazi-associated insignia – but does look back at the early days of the Nazis and the associated right-wing groups during the turbulent period of the Weimar Republic. However, the book makes no pretence at comprehensiveness simply because of the huge scale of the subject matter. Even though metal badges are beyond the remit of this volume, the history of cloth insignia in Nazi Germany itself is an immense and frequently controversial topic of study due to the huge number of badges produced during the period and the sometimes fragmentary or contradictory nature of the surviving evidence – and the abundance of misleading and often badly executed fakes. Nevertheless this book offers a sound introduction to the major cloth badges produced by the Third Reich, providing brief histories of the main organisations of the Nazi state and some of their most representative insignia, but it makes no claims to exhaustiveness or completeness. The photographs are used to highlight some of the more common badges of the period and indicate how and where they were worn.

The Nazi State and its Promotion

The overriding aim of Hitler and the Nazi Party hierarchy was totally to remould Germany in their image, to create a Third Reich based on national socialist ideology that was to last, as Hitler once boasted, for a thousand years. To achieve this immense ambition it was necessary to undertake a root-and-branch transformation of every aspect of the country's life from the state's administrative apparatus, through its economy, social structure and culture, to the everyday lives of its ordinary citizens. Existing structures, especially those tainted by association with the pre-Nazi Weimar Republic or non-Nazi bodies, were in some cases simply swept away or otherwise radically overhauled and moulded into National Socialist organisations, while scores of new offices were also created to implement key areas of Hitler's national and international political policies. No

BELOW: **Generalfeldmarschall Model (left), commander-in-chief of an army group fighting on the Eastern Front, in conversation with the commanding general of an armoured corps. Both wear peaked caps but the one worn by the commanding general (right) is the correct pattern for the Army officers' old style field service cap with its flat, machine-woven insignia. The other cap, bearing metal insignia, appears to be a normal uniform cap (Schirmmütze) but worn without cap cords.**

6

one, whether German or foreign, was to be left in any doubt that the Nazis had transformed the Weimar Republic into the Third Reich and that they had absolute control over the overall direction and running of the new state. A term was coined for the process of Nazification of Germany – Gleichschaltung, meaning co-ordination or unification of the political will – and the policy was immediately implemented on Hitler's assumption of power in January 1933 through wide-ranging government legislation that effectively brought pre-existing and independent bodies, such as the judiciary and trade unions, into the Nazi fold. Inevitably, the strength of the Third Reich was to be reflected, and its power demonstrated, by the administration's promotion of an all-encompassing and uniform German nationalism – individualism was replaced by collectivism under the Nazi banner. The supposed disorder engendered by the former was to be replaced by the order and discipline of the latter and thereby provide firm foundations for the future growth of the Third Reich.

Promotion of the Nazi Party and the Third Reich took many forms – mass party events, such as the rallies at Nuremberg held periodically between 1923 and 1938 (the latter attended by one million people), international events, including the 11th Olympic Games held in Berlin during 1936, and regular national events, including annual public holidays to celebrate, for example, National Labour Day (1 May) and Hitler's birthday (20 April) – and the process undoubtedly intensified once Hitler had become the country's head of state in 1934. However, the promotion of Nazism was not solely confined to the mass spectacles mentioned above; it also reached down to the level of the individual. The greater majority of Germans, at least those not considered undesirable, were in some way involved in promoting this aggressive nationalism by being identified with the Nazi Party, its leadership and the state it was transforming. From youth to old age, the Nazis ensured that ordinary Germans reflected their vision in some tangible way. This commitment

ABOVE: **Deputy Gauleiter Görlitzer of Berlin in conversation with Army personnel, all of whom had recently been fighting on the Eastern Front, March 1943.**

ABOVE: **Ernst Raack, a Berliner and a member of the German Hockey Eleven, photographed before the Germany–Hungary hockey match, December 1938. Sewn to his jacket are three sports awards, one dated 1937, plus the German emblem of the Reich Sports Association.**

RIGHT: **High-ranking spectators at the German gymnastic and sports festival held at Breslau in July 1938. Second from left the Reichssportsführer von Tschammer und Osten; on his left Gauleiter and Senior President Josef Wagner. (See also page 114.)**

might run from the mundane – having a picture of Hitler on the living room wall or attending a public rally as a spectator, for instance – to active membership of any one or more of the innumerable official organisations and institutions run by the state, all of which had some form of uniform and identifying insignia. Most German citizens acquiesced in the process of lauding Nazism either through genuine commitment to National Socialist ideals, general satisfaction with the Nazi-inspired reduction in unemployment and the crackdown on social disorder, or through fear of what might happen if they were seen to reject or criticise the regime in any way. The simplest and most visual means of demonstrating this loyalty to the Third Reich and membership of the new state was publicly to display its symbols on flags, banners and, of course, the clothing worn to indicate membership of one of its branches.

The process of Gleichschaltung radically altered the public face of Germany, which was re-created from top to bottom along National Socialist principles. The Nazis were unparalleled bureaucrats, not always efficient but certainly single-minded in creating a labyrinthine state structure based on a myriad of administrative bodies at national, regional, and local levels. To take the Nazi Party itself as an example, Hitler ruled over successive ranks of administrators which in 1933 comprised in descending order of importance several Reichsleiter (chiefs of the national party with particular portfolios such as party membership or its treasury), nine Landesinspekteur each of whom administered four Gaue (regions), 36 (later increased due to annexations) district leaders known as Gauleiters, plus increasingly numerous Kreisleiter (heads of local councils), Ortsgruppenleiter (responsible for a town section), Zellenleiter in charge of a neighbourhood of four or five housing blocks, and Blockwart, the official in charge of a single block and effectively the bottom rung of the party hierarchy's formal leadership above the ordinary member, who was known as a Parteigenosse (party comrade). At the higher levels at least, numerous administrative sections and support staff ensured that each bureaucrat could conduct his affairs effectively thereby creating a vast

uniformed organisation that required for each member badges and insignia of party membership, rank, and branch of service.

When other official state bodies are included – the Wehrmacht (armed forces), the civil service, and the police, for example, it becomes clear that the Nazis faced a mammoth task in creating the symbols that identified the particular organisation and the wearer's position within it. Believing in the concept that a picture or image was worth a thousand words, the Nazis embarked on the task with great dedication. Consequently, thousands of individual badges and sets of new Nazi insignia were created and these were issued to the appropriate individuals in their millions. Thus the history of insignia within the Third Reich is necessarily complex due to the vast range of organisations involved – military, paramilitary, political, administrative, economic and social – and their bureaucratic structures, the numerous patterns of emblems introduced or modified from time to time (and frequently found side by side), and in some cases the fragmentary nature of the evidence available.

Nevertheless, certain general points can be made about the various types of cloth insignia and where they were worn on the body, although any definitive statements should be treated with caution as there were frequent variations from the norm. The badges themselves fall into several general and sometimes overlapping categories: national and organisational badges, shoulder straps and collar patches, cuff-titles, armbands, and various trade and proficiency insignia. Many conveyed a range of information, but this can be divided into two main areas. First, there was general information, such as the wearer's membership of a particular state organisation, and, second, the specific – details relating to that individual's position within the body, either on a temporary or permanent basis. As well as rank this could include unit, service detachment or assignment, length of service, geographical area, training, combat experience and length of membership of the organisation. Above all this complex detail, much of which would have been mostly incomprehensible to the ordinary citizen, the insignia discussed in these pages conveyed the visually powerful and potentially intimidating information that the wearer was an integral part of the structure of the Third Reich and had been invested with some level of authority by its leadership.

ABOVE: **Hitler and Röhm at one a Nuremberg rally. In the background giant banners dominate the Luitpold Arena.**

National and Organisational Badges

All members of a uniformed official body wore an emblem identifying their membership of the German state and/or one of its official organisations. In many cases both the state and organisational badges were one and the same but if different it was not uncommon to see both insignia worn at the same time on different parts of the uniform. The national emblem during the Third Reich comprised an eagle, traditionally Germany's state symbol, to which was added a prominent Nazi swastika, the mark of the party, which was usually held in the eagle's talons and surrounded by a wreath. There was a wide variety of styles for both the eagle and wreath. Most commonly the somewhat stylised eagle was shown from the front with its head turned toward the right from the viewer's perspective, had outstretched and clipped, stepped wings, and held the wreathed swastika in both talons. However, this was not always the case. In contrast, the Luftwaffe eagle was more naturalistic, shown in part profile, and held an un-wreathed swastika in its right talon. Organisations that had an emblem markedly different from that of the Nazi state tended to have a badge that provided some indication of their function. Usually this consisted of a stylised device and the incorporation of abbreviated lettering representing the body's official title. For

ABOVE: **Reichsminister Dr Joseph Goebbels greeting members from the Panzergrenadier Division 'Feldherrnhalle' at his Berlin ministry. The troops saluting in the background are members of the SA-Standarte 'Feldherrnhalle'.**

example, the Nationalsozialistisches Flieger-Korps (NS Flying Corps) had a winged 'flying man' device probably based on the ancient Greek legend of Icarus, while the Deutsche Jägerschaft (German Hunter's Association) was identified by a stylised deer's skull with antlers and, unusually, also included a scroll with the lettering 'D.J.' Almost invariably, however, the organisational badge of such bodies also displayed the swastika.

The positioning, size and colour of the emblem varied. The three main branches of the Wehrmacht – Heer (Army), Kriegsmarine (Navy) and Luftwaffe (Air Force) – carried their organisational badges, which were essentially the state emblem, on their right breast above any pocket if the tunic included one. Other organisations tended to wear their insignia on the upper arm at a point halfway between the shoulder and elbow. In the case of the Waffen-SS it appeared on the left arm and on the right for members of the Nationalsozialistisches Kraftfahrer-Korps (NS Motor Corps). Organisational emblems were also found on the lower left arm as was the case with the badge of the Reichsluftschutzbund (Reich Air Defence League), which comprised the profile of an eagle in flight holding a swastika on a sunburst motif in its talons. With regard to size, there was some variation in these types of insignia but by no means as much as other types. Most had a width of around 10 cm and depths of approximately 4 cm excluding any backing cloth, although some designs were noticeably wider or deeper. Colours showed similar variation, although silver-white and gold-yellow were most common and were sometimes used to differentiate between other ranks/enlisted men (generally the former) and officers (the latter). Some organisations made use of other colours – the Hitler Youth lozenge with superimposed swastika consisted of unequally sized red and white quarters, for example. Where appropriate, the national and organisational symbols were manufactured on a background piece of cloth that was coloured to blend in with the tunic on which the insignia was worn. Field grey, blue-grey, dark navy blue, black and tan brown were most commonly used.

Shoulder Straps and Collar Patches

Shoulder straps and colour patches were probably the most important badges worn during the period of the Third Reich as they performed numerous functions that combined to indicate a person's status, function and position within the state. As with many other countries they indicated an individual rank or groups of ranks but the information frequently went farther. Additions were used to provide details of the wearer's unit. These ranged from numerals to short words or abbreviations. For example, members of the Army's 'Grossdeutschland' formation, which grew from regimental to divisional strength during World War II, were identifiable by the lettering GD. However, there was an enormous range of styles and combinations of shoulder straps and collar patches and many organisations introduced various patterns during the period of the Third Reich to complicate matters further.

Shoulder straps and collar patches were worn in a variety of ways, often together but this was by no means always the case, and many other combinations and styles existed. They could be worn in matching pairs (as was the case in the Heer, Kriegsmarine and Luftwaffe), but this system was not always followed by other formations. The straps or patches might be worn singly, shoulder straps might be omitted altogether, as was the case with the political leadership of the Nazi Party itself, or they might convey different information. It was common to find shoulder strap designs created to indicate groups of ranks worn with collar patches that identified on the one hand the wearer's actual rank and on the other his or her unit or attachment. In the case of the Allgemeine-SS (General SS) the right hand collar patch was used for the unit while the left showed rank up to a certain level.

BELOW: **Somewhere on the Eastern Front this small group of German infantry pause for a glass of wine, September 1942.**

11

OPPOSITE, ABOVE: **A variety of cuff-titles. From the top: three examples of German Army cuff-titles – the Secret Field Police title (Geheime Feldpolizei); the Army Propaganda Company title (Propagandakompanie); cuff-title worn by members of the Army Field Post service (Feldpost). All are manufactured by the same woven process and all are in silver-aluminium threads on black bands.**

Next three are: machine-woven version of the Feldgendarmerie (Field Police) cuff-title; a rare BeVo quality version of the 'Feldherrnhalle' cuff-title as worn by members of that division. Next the cuff-title worn by Marine-Küstenpolizei, the Naval Coastal Police.

These are followed by examples of elite German Army insignia – the copperplate lettered version of the Grossdeutschland cuff-title; the German handwritten script form of the Führer Headquarters cuff-title; the German handwritten script form of the Grossdeutschland cuff-title; a pair of rare Führer Begleit (Escort) Battalion shoulder straps for the lowest rank of Grenadier. These black cloth shoulder straps with white piping and white entwined letters 'GD' were worn with the German script Grossdeutschland cuff-title on the right cuff and the Führerhauptquartier cuff-title on the left cuff.

OPPOSITE, BELOW: **A seasoned German veteran of the fighting in North Africa and Sicily seen here at a prisoner-of-war camp at Palaia, Italy, November 1944. He wears the 'Afrika' with palms cuff-title awarded to him for his service in the Afrikakorps.**

Piping along the edges of the shoulder straps was also used to convey information about the wearer's parent organisation. Based on geographical divisions, the Hitlerjugend had several regional groups known as Oberbann and each was colour-coded – red, for example, identified Oberbann 1. The system was extended to include Hitler Youth members living outside Germany. Green identified those living in Asia, yellow North or South America, blue Africa and white Australia. One of the most common aspects of shoulder straps and collar patches were Waffenfarbe (branch of service) colours. The Luftwaffe, for example, used a system of Waffenfarbe to indicate membership of its various subdivisions. These included red for anti-aircraft units, yellow for flying personnel, light brown for signals, and black for construction. These colours appeared as piping on the shoulder straps and as the background colour of the collar patches and, with the addition of various other colours, symbols and so forth, provided details of rank, status and attachments. The Army followed a similar system as did the Reich's various police forces, in which membership of one of the various branches was indicated by what were known as Truppenfarben.

Cuff-Titles

Cuff-titles, narrow bands of cloth worn on both the left and right arm, were a frequent addition to sets of Nazi regalia, and entitlement to wear such badges was closely regulated by the authorities. Most titles were around 33 mm in width, although some were slightly wider or narrower. If the wearer was entitled to wear more than one title, then the earliest was worn above any subsequent awards. In certain cases, there was a distinction between the cuff-titles worn by officers and men. Generally, the former wore better quality titles which had any lettering or symbols hand-embroidered onto them, while the latter were provided with titles that were machine-embroidered. Different thread types and colours were also used to differentiate between the two groups of ranks. Although the distinction was not absolute, and variations were common, officers' titles had silver-aluminium or gold thread, while other ranks made do with grey-white cotton thread.

The bands themselves came in a variety of colours; some were manufactured with contrasting edgings while others were plain, and various forms of lettering were used. Black was the most common colour used for the cloth, although many Luftwaffe units entitled to wear cuffs had them in grey-blue cloth that matched their uniform. Brown, green, red and white fabrics were also used in producing some titles. Edgings were of two types – some were stitched onto the background cloth while others were woven directly into the cuff-title during production. The edgings were found in several positions from the very extremities of the cloth band to various positions within it. Again colours varied; although silver-white was the most common, other examples used gold-yellow and black. Lettering styles most commonly seen were Gothic, Roman, and Sutterlin, a type of German hand-written script, although Cyrillic was also used in certain instances. The style of the lettering could be either all capitals or a mixture of upper and lower case. Some titles carried additional embellishments. for example, the cuff-title produced for former Condor Legion personnel who had served during the Spanish Civil War contained the word 'Spanien', which was surrounded by the dates 1936 and 1939, while the Kurland campaign title issued in early 1945 carried two heraldic shields, one of which comprised the black cross of the Grand Masters of the Order of Teutonic Knights and the other contained an elk's head, the symbol of Kurland's one-time capital Mitau (now Jelgava), positioned either side of the word Kurland.

As with other emblems, cuff-titles performed numerous functions that served to provide a degree of information on the wearer. Several broad categories can be identified. First there were titles that identified a unit's official title, usually its name, or a commemorative title that had been added to its more mundane official designation. The latter was particularly common in the Luftwaffe, in which several units carried additional titles that commemorated famous German aces of the past, such as Max Immelmann, the World War I ace known as the 'Eagle of Lille' who was killed in 1916 with 15 victories to his credit. Other units bore titles that commemorated individuals who had achieved supposedly heroic status in the service of the Nazi Party. One of the most common was Horst Wessel, a young Nazi Party supporter killed by a communist, possibly a rival for his girlfriend's affection, in 1930, whose story was mythologised by party propagandist Joseph Goebbels. Such titles were particular popular with members and units of the SA and included such Nazi-approved figures as Albert Leo Schlageter, a young Freikorps member who was tried and executed by the French for espionage and sabotage in 1923 during the occupation of the Ruhr that followed Germany's announcement that it could no longer pay the war indemnities demanded in the provisions of the Treaty of Versailles.

Second, there were titles that reflected the wearer's broad area of service or attachment. Typical of these were titles bearing names such as Feldgendarmerie (Military Police), Bahnschutzpolizei (Railway Protection Police), or Führerhauptquartier (Führer headquarters). In the last case, permission to wear the title, which at 4 cm was one of the widest, was withdrawn once the individual had ended his attachment and been transferred elsewhere. Third, other cuff-titles commemorated the wearer's participation in a particular campaign and these were open to personnel from all of the Wehrmacht's branches – Air Force, Army and Navy – and were sometimes extended to individuals of other uniformed services. Strict rules were usually enforced to ensure an individual's entitlement to wear such a device. For example, the 'Afrika' cuff-title instituted in early 1943 for service in North Africa was open to anyone who had served six months in the theatre or three months if taken ill, or who had been wounded or decorated without achieving these lengths of overseas service. Unlike other types of cuff-title, no distinction was made between officers and men – all received the same type and quality of insignia.

Armbands

Armbands were one of the most common forms of insignia worn during the Nazi period and were provided not only for uniformed but also non-uniformed personnel who were performing some state function, often in an emergency. The wearing of the band in the latter case gave the individual temporary authority or identified his or her immediate status. For uniformed personnel the bands were often an integral part of the uniform and its insignia or could again denote a temporary attachment or emergency service. Bands worn in both of these cases, for both uniformed and non-uniformed individuals, were often surrendered to higher authority when the relevant crisis or period of service ended as they effectively belonged to the state not the individual. Bands that were an integral part of the uniform were retained by the wearer and worn whenever appropriate.

Armbands were produced in a variety of ways and their finish and quality varied enormously, although those that formed an integral part of the uniform were of generally higher quality than items that were issued in response to an emergency. As with other insignia, the quality of finish in general declined as the

ABOVE: **German Army Chaplain administering prayers to Russian children, July 1941. Clergy were employed in the ranks of the German Army for the religious well being of the troops. There were two grades of Army clergy, that of Army Chaplain and Senior Army Chaplain who wore insignia and tunic buttons in silver, and Field Bishops who had gold-coloured insignia and buttons. Both grades wore appropriate coloured collar patches but neither wore shoulder straps. The white and purple armband with a central red cross not only distinguished the wearer as a Roman Catholic priest or a Protestant minister but also afforded him protection as a non-combatant under the terms of the Geneva Convention.**

war turned decisively against the Third Reich. For example, many of the hastily raised Volkssturm home defence units created from late 1944 were issued with crudely stencilled armbands often produced locally and in haste to denote their official military status. The various types of bands were manufactured in a range of ways – they were machine-woven, details were embroidered by hand on to a cloth band, some were printed using silk screens or hand-stencilled, while others were roughly hand-written.

Armbands appeared in a variety of styles: single or multi-coloured, with or without symbols and lettering, and of various widths, but were invariably worn on the upper left sleeve, with the top of the band positioned midway between the elbow and shoulder and the lower edge resting on the elbow joint. Widths varied considerably but most fell in a range between approximately 12.5 cm and 7.5 cm, but with wider measurements being the more popular. Depending on their complexity, they provided various information, such as rank, temporary or permanent status, or branch of service. The most complex system of armbands belonged to the Nazi Party leadership itself and, under dress regulations introduced shortly before World War II, 38 variations of the standard Nazi red, white and black swastika armband were used to identify various grades of responsibility through combinations of differently coloured and positioned bands, edgings, and other embellishments such as oak leaves.

The design of armbands varied enormously but the most popular device to be included was the swastika, which almost invariably appeared in black. The German eagle was also common and frequently was combined with the swastika, while many other bands included the relevant organisational badge or lettering to indicate the wearer's unit. Although the Nazis created their own heraldry for

inclusion on badges, they also made use of more traditional, internationally recognised symbols. Chief among these was the Red Cross for medical personnel, which usually appeared with the lettering 'Deutsches Rotes Kreuz' and possibly details of the wearer's area of service.

Proficiency, Trade and Rank Badges

These types of cloth badges were particular to the individual wearer and indicated his or her qualifications or experience. Trade badges were awarded to those who worked in a particular area, such as medicine, administration or training, for example, while skill badges were awarded to those who had been specifically trained to perform a somewhat specialist function, such as sniping for infantry or range-finding for artillery. Rank badges were usually chevrons or bars – or combinations of both – to indicate status and were often seen with other trade or proficiency insignia, which were directly incorporated into the overall design. In the case of chevrons, the additional insignia were worn above and between the upper edges of the chevrons themselves. The trade and proficiency badges came in a wide range of styles. They varied in size as did the shape of the background cloth patch. Lozenges, circles, ovals, triangles, and shields were the most popular forms, but other designs including bands, oblongs and arrows were produced. As was common practice, the background cloth was generally the same colour as the uniform worn by the holder of the award, although this was not always the case and lighter and darker hues, or even completely different colours, were seen. Most common were black, light brown, grey-blue and field grey to echo the most widely seen tunics. The Kriegsmarine tended to have two background colours for its

ABOVE: **A German sailor, a guest on board an Italian destroyer, is invited to look through a pair of high-powered naval binoculars. Note the badges on his sleeve – the lower specialty badge, the chevrons of rank and the star indicating his career (Laufbahn).**

ABOVE: **The Army-pattern Feldgendarmerie duty gorget, worn by a Fallschirmjäger member of the Luftwaffe Field Police on traffic duty somewhere on the Eastern Front.**

badges – a dark navy blue to match the winter or temperate uniforms or white for the tropical or summer rig.

Details on the badges varied enormously but generally fell into three categories – lettering, recognisable symbols, or stylised designs. Script, mostly commonly Gothic or Roman, was often abbreviated to one or two letters. For example, the Gothic letter F might stand for Festungsbau (Army fortress construction) or Feuerwerk (Luftwaffe ordnance), although confusion was avoided by different background cloth – field grey for the former and blue-grey for the latter. Recognisable symbols usually had some association with the wearer's trade or skill and many were long established. Medical personnel made use of the serpent and staff motif while musicians were seen with a lyre emblem. Engineering and construction workers were awarded badges that often comprised the traditional tools of their trade, such as trowels, spanners, two-handed saws and axes. Stylised designs popular in the Third Reich were runic symbols, particularly the slanting, lightning bolt S and the three-armed Y. The designs were produced with a variety of thread types and colours but silver-white and gold-yellow were the most popular. Different colours or quality of finish on the insignia were often used to denote more senior status or experience as was the addition of cord-like edgings. Subtle variations in the basic design could also indicate greater experience. For example, sailplane examiners of the National Socialist Flying Corps, a cover organisation to prepare young Germans for Luftwaffe service, wore circular blue-grey badges with a stylised white aircraft within a similarly coloured broken cog wheel but variations in the wing design were used to differentiate between grades.

Trade and proficiency badges were worn on various parts of the uniform tunic but most commonly on the left or right forearm usually about 3.5–5 cm above the cuff. However, there were exceptions, Reichsarbeitsdienst (Reich Labour Service) personnel were identified by a Dienststellenabzeichen (service position badge) consisting of a shovel-like device that was carried on the upper left arm about half way between elbow and shoulder, while members of the Hitler Youth who had passed through the Reichsführerschule (Reich Leadership School) were permitted to wear a device above their right breast pocket.

Design and Manufacture

Badges of the Third Reich were generally produced to high standards, although as the war progressed and the state's resources became over-stretched, there was a noticeable decline in quality, complexity, and finish. The Nazis and their insignia designers drew inspiration for their badges from many sources. Some were based on symbols associated with pre-Nazi Germany, such as the state eagle or the Litzen (collar patch bars) that were a long-standing indication of officer rank and had been developed by Prussia; others had links stretching much farther back in time, such as the runic symbols that were used by Germanic and Scandinavian peoples of the Dark Ages and early medieval period and were themselves originally of ancient Greek and Roman origin. The ubiquitous swastika, the supposedly most Nazi of all symbols, was of equally ancient lineage and, in fact, had been used by many other cultures around the world throughout recorded history. Its appropriation by right-wing nationalists in Germany, who chose to believe that the swastika was a purely Teutonic device (and therefore appropriately Germanic), dated back only as far as the immediate pre-World War I period. It was taken over by the Nazis in their early days and heavily promoted by their propaganda machine headed by Joseph Goebbels until it became synonymous with the party and later the Third Reich. It was combined with the long-established

German eagle to become the official emblem of the Third Reich in an attempt to link the new state with the old and thereby give the new regime, which had gained only 44 percent of all votes cast in the March 1933 election, a seemingly greater degree of legitimacy by suggesting a balance between progress and tradition that was acceptable to most German citizens.

The Nazis turned to established artists and designers, such as Egon Jantke, to produce the blueprints for their badges, but took great pains to ensure that they came up with devices that were appropriate enough to reflect both the party and the state, often by melding together traditional symbols and colours, such as the red, white and black of the traditional German national flag, with those directly associated with the party. Once the design had been officially approved, the emblem was put into production at any one of numerous factories that specialised in such work. These were dotted across Germany but among the most famous were Assmann and Sons based in Lüdenschied and which concentrated on designs in metal, Bandfabrik Ewald Vorsteher of Wuppertal, which focussed on high-quality insignia that were silk woven and were generically known by the trademark acronym BeVo, and C.E. Junker based in Berlin.

Several processes were used to produce cloth badges. Among the most common (and of the best quality) were hand- or machine-embroidered items stitched on to a cloth background or, less commonly, directly on to the uniform, and machine-woven badges produced on a continuous band of cloth. The threads used were of three main types: cotton, metallic or silk. Other processes used to produce insignia were silk-screen printing, stencilling, or even hand-painting, although the quality of such items was generally poorer than the aforementioned processes and often reflected either the emblem's short-lived specific or emergency use or the increasingly parlous nature of the Third Reich's resources.

BELOW: **A young women from Vienna, a member of a German Army signals unit, operating a teleprinter somewhere in the French capital. These females were distinguished as qualified telephonists and teleprinter operators by the use of the German Army trade patch of a lightning 'Blitz' in lemon yellow on a dark green cloth oval.**

Army

On 16 March 1935, Adolf Hitler reintroduced conscription, a move heralding the vast expansion of Nazi Germany's armed forces, the Wehrmacht, over the following four years. The new Heer (Army), chief beneficiary of the Nazi militarisation programme, was based around the professionals of the 100,000-strong inter-war Reichsheer that had been permitted under the provisions of the Treaty of Versailles and to these men were added recruits from the police, various paramilitary formations associated with the Nazis, volunteers and the conscripts themselves. Although few of these troops saw combat before World War II, by 1939 the German Army was a formidable force due to rigorous training and the high level of motivation and self-belief of all ranks. The Army consisted of five types of divisions – armoured, infantry, light, motorised, mountain – each with an initial strength of around 15–18,000 men and, although lacking certain equipment, their organisation, leadership and training were generally superior to those of their opponents. The Oberkommando des Heeres (OKH/Army High Command), which included the professionals of the general staff, had overall charge of the Army but Hitler increasingly came to distrust his senior officers and made himself commander-in-chief of the Army in late 1941, a decision that was to have an adverse effect on operations for the remainder of the war.

Nevertheless, between September 1939 and autumn 1941, the Army won a series of stunning Blitzkrieg victories across Europe but failed to engineer the surrender of Britain and the Soviet Union, strategic defeats that forced Germany to fight a war on two fronts. From 1943 the Army surrendered the initiative to the Allies and the days of triumph were over. Henceforth, until final defeat, it was generally on the defensive and faced numerically and materially stronger opponents. The Army was gradually bled white, particularly on the Eastern Front, and limited counter-attacks to stave off defeat rather than major offensives to win outright victory became the norm. Yet many of the troops continued to fight exceptionally well and demonstrated great defensive skills in the final two years of the conflict, even after the the realities of a two-front war were brought home by the D-Day landings in June 1944. Only in the very final days of the fighting did the Army's morale and fighting spirit collapse, with troops surrendering to the Allies in their tens of thousands. The German Army has been described as the 'motor' of the war, the driving force the Allies had to destroy to achieve victory, and as such its defeat was accompanied by heavy

BELOW: **A pair of collar patches as worn by an Armed Forces' administrative official (Wehrmachtbeamter) with the position of Oberintendanturrat (Senior Commissariat Councillor).**

losses among its own troops – an estimated 3.25 million men became casualties between 1939 and 1945.

As with all branches of the Wehrmacht the Army had a universal organisational badge which was worn above the right pocket of the tunic. It consisted of the national eagle emblem holding a wreathed swastika in its talons. The design appeared in silver-white on a dark green background, and was either machine-produced or hand-embroidered. Removable dark green shoulder straps performed several functions and were worn in pairs. First, they identified the wearer's branch of service by the addition of a fine coloured edging, the Waffenfarbe. Among these were white for infantry, salmon-pink for armour, black for engineers and bright red for artillery. With various additions of lettering, symbols and so forth, shoulder straps could also indicate various levels of officer rank, or membership of a particular unit, or function.

Collar patches, again worn in pairs, could also denote rank or branch of service. Generally, for ranks below non-commissioned level, they consisted of dark green cloth with traditional double bars (Litzen) in light grey separated by a darker grey line, while various additions of lace and other symbols were made for non-commissioned and full officers. For the various grades of ordinary soldiers, rank appeared only on the upper left arm as shoulder straps, while collar patches were generally

ABOVE: Oberstleutnant Graf von der Goltz, commander of a Mountain Troop regiment, offers his cigarette as a light for one of his soldiers. Von Goltz wears the Army officers' old style field service cap.

plain barring the Waffenfarbe and Litzen. Privates wore no badge, but others were identified by various designs on the upper left arm. A senior private (Oberschütze) was identified by a dark green oval with a central star, while non-commissioned officers wore designs comprising combinations of silver-white chevrons and stars on a dark green background.

Cuff-titles were worn by personnel for several reasons – to denote participation in an important or noteworthy campaign, membership of a particular unit, or service in a particular branch of the Army, for example – and were found on both the left and right forearms. They varied in width, although 33 mm was most common, and had numerous background colours; black, green, light brown and white being the most familiar. Edgings, again found in several colours, were often included in the design, while the main central motif comprised a title in either Roman or Gothic script possibly with further embellishment in the form of a

heraldic shield or other symbol relevant to what was being commemorated, particularly in the case of titles indicating participation in a campaign, and usually appearing on either side of the script. For example, North Africa (rendered 'Afrika' on the design) was symbolised by palm trees and pre-war service in Spain ('Spanien') with the Condor Legion by the addition of the dates 1936 and 1939. If a wearer was entitled to more than one such cuff-title the earliest would be worn above subsequent awards.

Trade badges usually appeared on the right forearm, although there were exceptions. Signallers, for example, wore theirs on the upper right sleeve, while artillery gunlayers carried them on the lower left sleeve. The badges themselves consisted of a dark green or khaki oval or circular patch that contained either a symbol or Gothic lettering (sometimes both) that indicated the wearer's status. The designs were usually rendered in yellow but were also found in salmon pink for personnel attached to armoured formations. A corded edge usually in the same colour as the emblem denoted higher grades. Arm badges were also worn by members of specialist formations, most notably by mountain troops, troops from rifle units trained in ski use, and the Army's Field Police, and appeared on either the upper left or upper right arm.

OPPOSITE, ABOVE: The early Wehrmacht Army sports vest emblem. This was worn sewn to the front of the white sports vests.

OPPOSITE, BELOW: Army officers and Army officials listen intently to a speech.

LEFT: Armband issued to, and worn by, those persons employed in the service of the Wehrmacht. Frequently these employed persons were civilians or foreigners and, under the terms of the Geneva Convention, in order that they were to be regarded as armed forces' personnel and not as fifth columnists, the wearing of this armband was essential. The black lettering on yellow band was standard issue but the addition of the rank insignia as here – a black-edged green bar indicating the wearer was an Unteroffizier – is unusual. Printed items such as this were normally worn on those garments that did not display ranks in the normal way, in other words clothing that didn't have collar patches or shoulder straps.

BELOW LEFT: Generaloberst Dietl talking with a senior Luftwaffe officer (left) and the commanding general of the Eismeerfront (the Arctic Front). Generaloberst Dietl is wearing a non-issue, heavy duty cold weather coat, on the upper arm of which he displays his rank by means of the special insignia introduced for wear on German Army camouflage and special combat clothing. Note, too, the mountain troops' Edelweiss on his cap.

ABOVE: **Two examples of the German Army Standard Bearer's arm shield – on the left that worn by a bearer from an infantry battalion and, on the right, one worn by a bearer from an armoured battalion. The difference was distinguished by the colour of the displayed Colours, white being the arm-of-service colour (Waffenfarbe, see glossary) for the infantry and rose pink for the armoured arm. These badges were worn on the right upper arm of bearers' tunics. Although the two badges are shown here as upright rectangles and are referred to as 'shields', when sewn to the tunic arm the edge around the design was tucked up and sewn to leave a badge with a shield-shaped outline.**

ABOVE RIGHT: **A pair of Army officer's field service collar patches, here those of an engineer officer. The matt silver-grey embroidery and the blue-green background show these to be field service patches. The twin lines of coloured twisted cording set between the double bars of embroidery indicate the wearer's arm-of-service – black for the Pioneers.**

RIGHT: **An example of the BeVo quality cap wreath and cockade for wear on the Army officer's old style field service cap (see photo at left and on page 19).**

ABOVE: **A pair of Panzer collar patches. Pink, or rosa, was the piping colour, the arm-of-service colour of the Panzer arm. Black was their uniform colour and the small silver metal skull was an historical emblem associated with Germany's Imperial Hussars.**

RIGHT: **A tank commander standing in the open turret of his vehicle. He wears the special black uniform worn by all German Army tank formations, with its collar patches, but wears the field grey old style field service cap. There was no black version of this cap for wear by Panzer troops and, as with their greatcoats, they wore standard issue field grey items.**

ABOVE LEFT: **Generaloberst Busch inspecting some of his troops. He is shown here shaking hands with a senior NCO – also called 'der Spiess' or 'mother of the company'.**

LEFT: **Unteroffizier Klose receiving the congratulations from his comrades on receiving the Knight's Cross of the Iron Cross.**

OPPOSITE, ABOVE: In Germany before and during the war those persons who were blind, in addition to carrying a white stick, could, if they wished, wear an identifying armband. A yellow armband with three solid black spots and a black Maltese cross indicated a person who had lost his or her sight whilst serving in the German armed forces. Civilians who had been blinded wore a similar band but without the cross.

OPPOSITE, BELOW LEFT AND RIGHT: Two versions of the cap insignia worn on the front of the 1943 pattern Einheitsfeldmütze or general issue field cap. The lower badge, with a black background, was for wear on the Panzer version of this cap; the upper version for wear on field grey caps.

RIGHT: The BeVo quality arm badge for wear by members of German Army Jäger troops.

BELOW: One of a number of the BeVo quality woven breast eagles. The firm of Ewald Vorsteher of Wuppertal manufactured its machine woven insignia as a continuous strip or band. It produced many designs, the one shown here is a breast eagle for wear by Army officers.

26

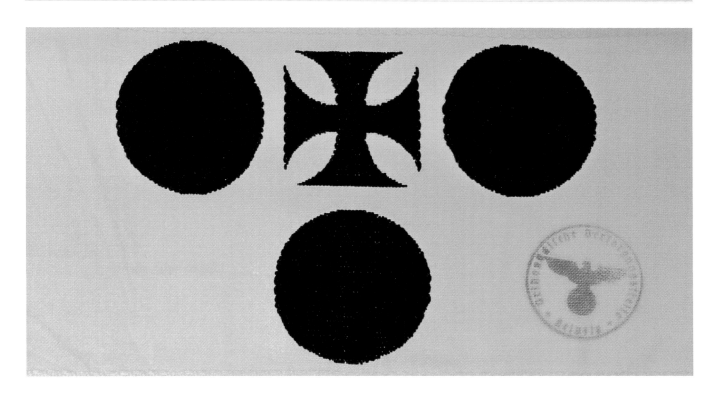

ABOVE: The BeVo breast eagle for wear by German Army troops wearing tropical uniform.

RIGHT: An unnamed general officer taken prisoner in Italy. He is a veteran of World War I, having been awarded both the 1st and 2nd class Imperial Iron Cross.

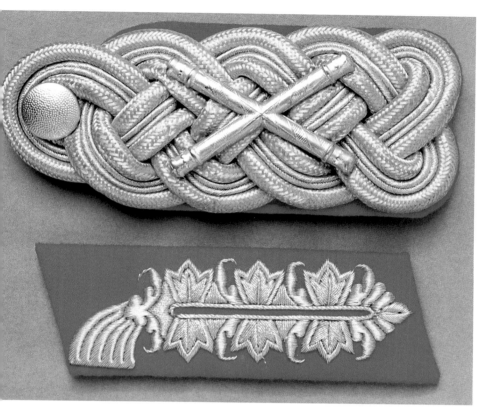

LEFT: Shoulder strap and collar patch for a field marshal (Generalfeldmarschall) of the German Army.

BELOW: A pair of shoulder straps and collar patches for a lieutenant-general (Generalleutnant) of the German Army.

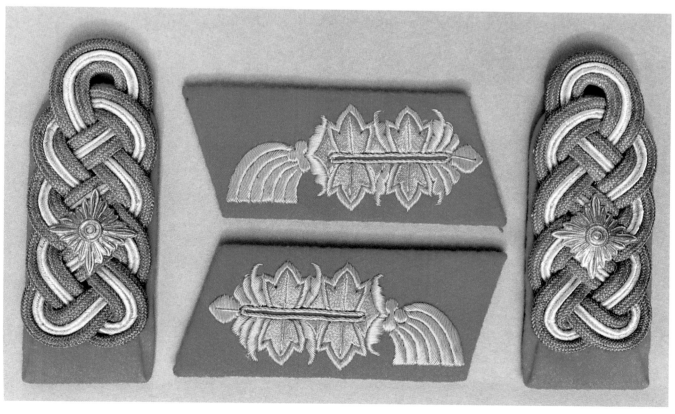

RIGHT: Officers and soldiers of Guard Troop Berlin look on as one of their number, wearing full marching order, performs a series of gruelling exercises, part of an endurance test undertaken to earn a military sports award. The physical training instructor in the centre of the photograph is wearing the Reichswehr/early Wehrmacht sports vest emblem.

BELOW RIGHT: An Army Obergefreiter range-taking. He wears double rank chevrons on his left upper arm and on his left cuff he displays the early Wehrmacht marksmanship insignia that was in use from 1920 to 1936, shown here as a single strip of flat 8 mm broad silver-aluminium braid. This indicates the first, and lowest, classification of marksman.

OPPOSITE, ABOVE LEFT: Brothers about to proceed on leave; both are in the German Army, the soldier on the right is serving with the German Panzer arm.

OPPOSITE, ABOVE RIGHT: An NCO from a German Army Field Police unit somewhere on the island of Crete. He wears the Feldgendarmerie duty gorget, his Field Police arm eagle, an orange embroidered eagle and wreath with a black swastika, and his grey-on-brown cuff-title.

OPPOSITE, BELOW: Crewmen of a German armoured vehicle talking with an admiring farm girl. This was probably taken in the first year of the war as all three men are still wearing the prewar Panzer beret. This was a form of protective headdress, the black cloth beret covering an inner protective helmet.

ABOVE: **An Army NCO Instructor of the Heereswaffenmeisterschule in Berlin checking the calibration made by a pupil. The staff of this and other German Army Armament Instruction Schools were distinguished by the use of 'WS' monograms carried on their shoulder straps.**

OPPOSITE, ABOVE: **German infantry somewhere on the Eastern Front. Both men wear slip-on loops on their shoulder straps. These had a particular significance within their unit but without knowing the colour of these cloth loops it is difficult to arrive at an explanation as to their purpose.**

OPPOSITE, BELOW LEFT: **An Army cameraman from a propaganda company. He would have a cuff-title such as that illustrated second from the top on page 13.**

OPPOSITE, BELOW RIGHT: **An unnamed Army Oberfeldwebel and holder of the Knight's Cross. This NCO wears the Engineer Assault Boat Helmsman badge on his left upper arm.**

LEFT: **Carrier pigeons in the service of the German Army being checked by an Oberbrieftaubenmeister, a senior Pigeon Post Master.**

Air Force

BELOW: As the war progressed and the tide began to turn against Germany Luftwaffe aircrew found themselves defending German airspace. If their aircraft was shot down and they succeeded in bailing out over German-held territory it was necessary to wear this special armband as a form of identification. Frequently, Luftwaffe crew members, in attempting to make their way to the nearest military unit, or those who landed injured and were in need of help, were mistaken by the local population as Allied airmen or at least mistaken for advancing enemy troops. To counter this misunderstanding aircrew were required to wear this special identification armband.

Although strictly forbidden an air force under the provisions of the Treaty of Versailles, Germany began creating a military aviation arm in the 1920s, secretly sending men to train as pilots in the Soviet Union. The process was intensified when the Nazis came to power under the cover of the pseudo-civilian Deutsche Luftsportsverband (DLV/German Air Sports Association), which offered training on gliders to potential pilots. The existence of the Luftwaffe (Air Force) as a fully independent branch of the Wehrmacht was made public in March 1935 by which time it comprised some 1,900 aircraft and 20,000 personnel chiefly trained on and flying aircraft designed to provide tactical close support for ground operations. Hermann Goering was made Nazi Germany's first air minister and head of the new force, a position he held for most of World War II despite his gradual fall from Hitler's favour. Expansion and the introduction of modern military aircraft were rapid and in 1937 the Luftwaffe began testing its Blitzkrieg tactics by supporting the Nationalists in the ongoing Spanish Civil War with its 'volunteer' Legion Kondor (Condor Legion).

By 1939 the Luftwaffe, which was also responsible for anti-aircraft and paratrooper units (the latter founded during 1935–36), consisted of 1.5 million personnel of whom 50,000 were aircrew, 80,000 in maintenance and supply, 125,000 in administration, and 60,000 in the construction branch – front-line

services dwarfed by the staggering 900,000 men earmarked for the Luftwaffe's anti-aircraft branch. The rest (some 300,000) were new recruits undergoing instruction.

Overall strategy was the responsibility of the Oberkommando der Luftwaffe (OKL/Luftwaffe High Command), which directed operations in support of the ground forces during the vast Blitzkrieg invasions of Poland, Western Europe, the Balkans and the Soviet Union between 1939 and 1941. Thereafter the Luftwaffe increasingly became a home-defence force, effectively part of the country's extensive anti-aircraft network, as the Anglo-American strategic bomber offensive against Nazi Germany moved into top gear from late 1942. Confronted by increasing enemy air superiority, and short of aircraft, trained pilots and fuel, it was ground down over the following two years and by 1945 had effectively ceased to exist as a significant fighting force. In similar fashion the Luftwaffe's paratrooper force scored some notable early successes that marked it out as an elite formation but, after suffering heavy losses during the battle of Crete in 1941, it was relegated to purely ground roles in which it continued to fight with distinction until the end of the war.

The Luftwaffe badge, found above the tunic's right breast pocket was a variant of the Nazi national symbol with the eagle in flight and holding the swastika in its talons. The officer

ABOVE: A Hauptmann (captain), a pilot who, according to the official caption, is also a Croatian volunteer serving in the Luftwaffe. On the right breast pocket of his tunic he wears the Ehrenzeichen der Kroatischen Legion (the Honour Badge of the Croatian Legion) directly below the Luftwaffe national emblem, and on his left breast pocket can be seen, edge on, the Croat pilot's badge.

version was embroidered in silver thread. Luftwaffe shoulder straps and collar patches, which grew out of those worn by members of the DLV and were introduced in March 1935, became increasingly complex and the matching pairs worn were used to identify an individual's rank, branch and unit. Branch of service was indicated by coloured edging on shoulder straps or the background on collar patches – yellow for aircrew, light brown for signals and red for anti-aircraft artillery, for example – and a secondary edging sometimes indicated a branch sub-division. For example, during the period early 1940–late 1941, dark green and yellow edging indicated a navigator officer of the flying branch. Lettering and other symbols on the shoulder straps and stylised wings, wreaths and other devices in silver thread on the collar patches were further used to indicate rank and branch of service. Rank was also identified by silver-white chevrons on blue patches carried on the upper left arm or, in the case of flying suits, by a series of stylised

ABOVE: **The Luftwaffe national emblem, another example of the BeVo style manufacture, which was worn on dark blue work clothing.**

wings and bars worn on both upper arms. The background colour for these rectangular cloth patches was usually the same as the flying suit, often light tan, while the symbols appeared either in white or gold-yellow depending on rank.

On occasion armbands were worn on the upper left arm. These performed a number of functions – some related to an individual's role, such as fire-fighting duties or interpreting, while others reflected assignments, such as membership of the Condor Legion or officer cadet school. Luftwaffe personnel were also permitted to wear titles on the right cuff. These consisted of two main types: first, those granted to personnel who were serving in a particular theatre, those wounded in the theatre but recovering elsewhere, or men of leave from the theatre; and second, those that simply identified a unit by name. In the former case the title was removed once service in the theatre was concluded. In the case of specific names, air groups were generally dedicated to the memory of deceased air aces, such as World War I's Manfred von Richthofen or, more rarely, Nazi icons such as Horst Wessel. The background colour for the cuff-titles was generally blue, or green for paratroopers, with silver lettering in either Gothic or Roman script, and in some cases titles had similar-coloured edging. The quality of the finish and design complexity varied with rank from ordinary soldiers, through non-commissioned grades to full officers.

As befitted a highly technical service, the Luftwaffe introduced numerous trade and proficiency badges. Emblems denoting specialist qualifications were worn on the left forearm of all types of uniform and appeared in a variety of shapes from flattened ovals to shield-like designs, although all had a blue background and usually silver embroidery and incorporated a pair of wings. Other elements, either brief lettering or a symbol, indicated the particular speciality. A twisted gold edging indicated 12 months of experience in a particular field. Similarly, the Luftwaffe had numerous trade and proficiency badges, some 36, and these were overwhelmingly worn on the left forearm although occasionally found on the

ABOVE: **A similar quality national emblem for wear on green or camouflage clothing.**

LEFT: **Intense concentration as these two Luftwaffe officers instruct an infantry unit about the position for an air drop. The officer on the left is wearing the Legion Kondor cuff-title that indicated he was a member of the Kampfgeschwader 53 'Legion Kondor'.**

upper left arm or right forearm. The designs comprised a blue circle with mostly silver-white designs. As with specialist qualifications, these emblems were generally letters or symbols. For example a Verwaltungsunteroffizier (administrative non-commissioned officer) was identified by a Gothic letter V, while communications personnel were generally identified by some form of stylised lightning bolt.

OPPOSITE: **Romanian and German Air Force officers, July 1944. The Romanian officer on the right is General Jonescu, holder of the German Knight's Cross. The German officer on the left is wearing the commemorative cuff-title awarded to those persons who had served during the World War I in the Jagdgeschwader Richthofen.**

LEFT: **The Luftwaffe national emblem, hand-embroidered, gold bullion quality for wear by officers and officials of general rank.**

BELOW LEFT: **The Luftwaffe national emblem, hand-embroidered in silver wire bullion for wear by all officers and officials below the rank of general.**

RIGHT: **The Luftwaffe national emblem, early pattern. It is hand-embroidered in white threads. The design of the national emblems used during the first years of the Luftwaffe tended to have the tail feathers of the eagle curling down. This is very noticeable when compared with the top illustration on the next page.**

BELOW: **Three highly decorated members of the same bomber crew, photographed in June 1944 somewhere on the Western Front. Left to right: bomber squadron commander Oberstleutnant Hogeback with his air gunner, Oberfeldwebel Glasner, and his wireless operator, Oberfeldwebel Lehnart. All three men wear the Bomber Operational Flying Clasp with the star pendant for having flown a minimum of 300 sorties. Oberfeldwebel Glasner wears the Krim (Crimea) campaign arm shield, and the Kreta and Afrika with palms campaign cuff-titles on his left forearm.**

LEFT: **A late war production of the ubiquitous Luftwaffe breast eagle. Note that this is machine woven in silver-aluminium threads and has an overlocked, stitched edging, a method that helps prevent fraying.**

BELOW: **A German paratrooper standing duty in a slit trench somewhere on the southern sector of the Eastern Front. He wears his Kreta campaign cuff-title on the left forearm of his tunic.**

ABOVE: This colour illustration gives an excellent comparison in size of the standard issue, machine-embroidered, other ranks' quality national emblem (upper) and the emblem as worn on a Luftwaffe officer's cloak.

RIGHT: Telephone operators of the Luftnachrichten-Helferinnenschaft (air reporting-female helpers' team). All wear rank insignia on the left upper sleeve of their blue-grey jackets and above which they display their trade badge.

ABOVE LEFT: A medical officer treats the wounds of a young Unteroffizier fighter pilot, October 1943. The arm-of-service colour appointed for the Luftwaffe medical branch was dark blue.

ABOVE: An Oberfeldwebel inspecting and testing the compressed-air bottle for inflating a rubber dingy. The trade badge on his left forearm is that for flight technical personnel (Fliegertechnisches Personal).

LEFT: Knight's Cross holder Major Herbert Kaminski (seated in deck chair) photographed when he was commander of I/JG53.

RIGHT AND BELOW RIGHT: **Two versions of the national emblem for wear on the front of the Luftwaffe flight cap. The upper one has a backing of black material and was intended to be worn on the black fatigue cap. The lower badge incorporates the cockade of the German national colours.**

BELOW: **Three Luftwaffe cuff-titles. The upper item was the formation cuff-title worn by those Luftwaffe troops serving in the North African theatre of operations. The version shown here was worn by men and NCOs. It had off-white lettering on a dark blue band. The following two cuff-titles, both of green cloth, were for wear by personnel of Parachute Regiment 1. The central title had grey cotton lettering and was worn by other ranks. The lower one was with silver metallic lettering and silver-grey Russia braided edging. This was the quality worn by officers of the regiment.**

OPPOSITE: **Rank was displayed on protective flight clothing by a system of arm badges that consisted of stylised wings, bars and pips (in white or yellow), with the most senior ranks of Oberstgeneral and Generalfeldmarschall having oval wreaths combined with the Luftwaffe national emblem. The rank worn here was that for an Oberst (colonel).**

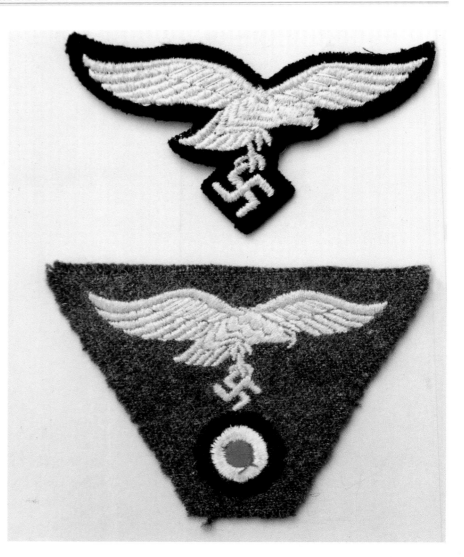

Navy

The strength of the Kriegsmarine (German Navy) was severely restricted by the Treaty of Versailles in 1919 and, although its provisions prohibited the building of submarines, aircraft carriers, naval aircraft, coastal artillery and ships over 10,000 tons, Hitler initiated an expansion programme in the 1930s. A major step forward came with the signing of the Anglo-German Naval Treaty in June 1935, which allowed the Kriegsmarine to increase its strength to 35 percent of the Royal Navy's and swept away the restrictions imposed at the end of World War I. In 1938 a wholesale expansion programme known as Plan Z began with the intention of giving Germany naval parity with Britain by 1945, but this construction drive was curtailed with the outbreak of war as resources were directed elsewhere. Nevertheless, the Kriegsmarine fielded some 37 major surface ships and 56 U-boats in September 1939 and by 1941 it had a total strength of some 400,000 personnel.

The Kriegsmarine had three major divisions, each commanded by a Führer (leader) – major surface vessels, which were directly controlled by the naval high command, the Oberkommando der Marine (OKM), smaller warships such as minesweepers and coastal defence vessels, which were attached to the naval security section, and the submarine branch. The Kriegsmarine did not have an aviation branch and a senior Luftwaffe liaison officer known as the Führer der Marineluftstreitkräfte (leader of naval air forces) was charged with satisfying the Navy's aircraft needs. Overall leadership of the Kriegsmarine lay with Grand Admiral Erich Raeder between 1935 and 1943 and with Admiral Karl Dönitz from the latter date until the end of the war. Raeder's dismissal and Dönitz's appointment reflected the different fortunes of the Kriegsmarine's two main branches. By 1943 the surface fleet had suffered severe losses, and many of the remaining vessels lay in harbour making little effort to interrupt the flow of supplies to Britain from the United States across the North Atlantic. Only Dönitz's command, the U-boat flotillas, appeared capable of stemming the flow and the submarine offensive became the cornerstone of Germany's naval strategy for the reminder of the war. In January 1943 Hitler ordered the cancellation of the surface warship building programme and all available resources were focussed on U-boat construction. Some 1,160 U-boats were ultimately built, and caused the Allies major problems until the very final days of the conflict, but never quite succeeded in starving Britain into submission and suffered increasing losses from the summer of 1943. Of the total U-boat force, 785 were destroyed, while 156 were scuttled and the remainder surrendered in 1945. Crew casualties were also extremely high; some 32,000 men were killed out of a total of 39,000 who served.

BELOW: Standing in the conning tower of his U-boat an Obersteuermann takes a sextant bearing from the sun. The small badge worn on the side of his cap was an unofficial insignia that displayed the unofficial symbol or design of his U-boat flotilla or his own U-boat. These badges used designs that were sometimes replicated on conning towers or other locations.

As with all of Nazi Germany's Wehrmacht (armed forces), members of the Kriegsmarine carried badges indicating their branch of service, rank, trade, and skill or proficiency on their various tunics, which were of either dark blue for standard wear or white for summer and tropical service. The national emblem was carried above the tunic's right breast pocket, and comprised the German eagle holding the Nazi swastika in its talons on a dark blue background to match the colour of naval clothing. Commissioned officers' eagles appeared in gilt, while the other ranks' version was manufactured in yellow thread. Officer rank was also identified by embroidery on the cap peak, gold lace cuff rings of varying number and width on reefer jacket cuffs, and sometimes by shoulder straps, although the latter were only worn by commissioned and warrant officers, midshipmen, administrative personnel and musicians. Collar patches, which like shoulder straps only appeared on certain uniforms, were worn in pairs by petty officers, ordinary seamen and clergy. Shoulder straps for officers comprised a blue background, silver or gilt thread (or a combination of both) and various silver or gilt badges. Collar patches were often just plain blue, although petty officers carried additional yellow bands; two in the case of an Obermaat (chief petty officer).

In addition, ranks below officer level also wore various badges on the upper left arm. Petty officers were identified by a yellow thread anchor and senior petty officers by an additional chevron below the anchor, and various designs were produced to indicate a particular trade. An anchor incorporating two crossed quill pens was used to identify a writer petty officer. Leading and able seamen were similarly identified by yellow chevrons on the upper left arm that increased in number or complexity of design with rank and length of service. The wearer's department of service badge often appeared within the chevron badge.

ABOVE: **War badges were introduced into the German forces to identify the wearer's branch of service whilst at the same time rewarding the recipient for service in his chosen branch. There were complicated rules regulating the award of these war badges and those that were awarded were always in metal, some representing greater achievements having brilliants or diamond chips added to the design.**

Metal war badges, however, were not always convenient to wear and thus cloth versions of the badges were produced that could be worn in their place. The designs followed closely the original metal items and the coloured metals were copied on the cloth versions in silver-grey and yellow coloured threads.

Left shows the cloth version of the Kriegsmarine Destroyer War Badge (Zerstörer-Kriegsabzeichen), and right that of the High Seas Fleet War Badge (Flotten-Kriegsabzeichen).

LEFT: **The naval rate badge for a petty officer. This is an early Kriegsmarine badge and one of the very few that incorporated a coloured emblem on the standard badge, in this case the red Roman letter 'V' standing for Verwaltung (supply) on the yellow anchor.**

RIGHT: **The naval rate badge for a signals petty officer. The standard badge for this rate produced in gilt coloured metal, and as with other metal rate badges, was usually worn on dress and walking out uniforms. This item has crossed signal flags, which indicated the wearer was a qualified signaller. It is of interest to note that the flags attached to the gilt metal flag staffs are machine embroidered in red and white cotton threads. These flags represent, in naval signalling parlance, the letter 'C'.**

A wide range of small oval arm badges on a dark blue background was also carried to show the wearer's Laufbahn (career badge). Officers' versions indicating branch of service appeared on the forearms above the sleeve rings previously mentioned and came in several designs: line officers had a gilt thread five-pointed star and engineers a cog wheel, for example. Officer cadets undergoing training wore similar badges with the addition of an edging in twisted gold thread representing coiled ropes, while civilian officials attached to the Navy wore badges with silver-white thread. Those serving for the duration of the war were further identified by a similarly coloured edging representing a single length of twisted rope. Department-of-service badges for those below officer level who had completed basic training were worn on the upper left arm above any rank insignia and consisted of various designs in coloured thread on a usually dark blue background, although for summer wear the badges appeared in blue thread on a white cloth background. The designs incorporated symbols appropriate to the particular trade. Carpenters were identified by a measuring compass and signallers by a pair of crossed semaphore flags, for example.

Ordinary seamen who had acquired specialist skills were also issued with a range of oval badges that were worn on their left arm below any badges of rank and department of service emblems. The badges appeared in red silk thread on both dark blue and white (summer) oval cloth backgrounds. The designs, often highly stylised, came in many representational forms, such as torpedoes, propellers, and diving helmets, and might also include an indication of length of service or seniority.

BELOW LEFT: Anti-submarine operations. The 'BU' or Befehlsübermittler (literally command transmitter) awaiting instructions from the bridge of his destroyer. The single yellow chevron indicated, after January 1938, the rank of Gefreiter. The five-pointed star (the Laufbahn, or career badge) worn directly above the chevron shows this man was following a career as a boatswain.

BELOW: An Obergefreiter, indicated by two yellow chevrons, on duty on board a torpedo boat somewhere off the coast of Norway. The white metal skull worn on the side of his service cap was the semi-official emblem adopted by the crew of this torpedo boat or it may have been the emblem of the entire torpedo boat flotilla.

OPPOSITE, ABOVE: **The tropical version of the German national emblem worn on naval tan-coloured tropical clothing.**

OPPOSITE, BELOW: **The national emblem for wear on naval white clothing.**

ABOVE: **A version of the national emblem for wear on the normal dark navy blue clothing.**

LEFT: **A reception was held in Berlin to welcome home members of the armed forces who had been engaged in operations in the Indian Ocean off Madagascar. Leutnant Witte, the centre of attention, had just returned from his U-boat operational cruise along the southern coast of the island.**

RIGHT: The standard, hand embroidered version of the Kriegsmarine national emblem. This quality could be worn both by officers or ratings, in the case of the latter usually on their best uniform.

OPPOSITE: A U-boat petty officer emerges from below deck prior to disembarking from this Royal Navy warship at an unspecified port in the United Kingdom at the start of his journey to a prisoner of war camp. It would seem from the amount of gear he is carrying, not to mention his cap and leather coat, that he must have had time allowed to him before he was forced to abandon his boat.

BELOW: Members of a ship's company of a German warship spend a peaceful Christmas aboard their vessel in the first year of the war, 1939. All the men, with the obvious exception of the petty officer, are wearing their best white uniforms.

RIGHT: A pair of collar patches of the second pattern for wear by a clergyman with over two years' naval war service as a naval padre (Marinekriegspfarrer v.2 Jahr ab Marinepfarrer) or by a senior naval padre (Marineoberpfarrer). Similar collar patches but with the embroidery work and twisted cording around the edge in gold threads were worn by senior German naval deacons (Dienstälteste Marine Dekane).

BELOW: Three cuff-titles with German naval associations. The upper two were worn by Naval Hitler Youth and as their lettering implies, they were worn by naval helpers. The lower title was worn by uniformed females serving in the German Navy as office personnel.

ABOVE: Female naval personnel POWs head to the mess hall. They are wearing a variety of civilian and military dress and only two have the correct uniform, side-cap and cuff-titles on the left sleeves.

LEFT: A youthful looking sailor wearing the plain blue collar patches indicating the lowest grade of seaman, that of Matrose.

RIGHT: **A member of the Naval Hitler Youth being presented with flowers by a woman member of the Reichsarbeitsdienst on the occasion of the ninth anniversary of compulsory service in the RAD. This youth from a unit in East Prussia, together with the others in this photograph, is about to be drafted into the RAD.**

BELOW: **This photo clearly shows the three sets of collar patches worn in the German Navy by the lower ranks of Matrose worn without collar braiding (far left), Obermaat (next) and Maat (far right). Both these two latter ranks wear gilt, one-centimetre wide collar braiding. Without seeing their rate badges it is not possible to ascertain their careers.**

LEFT: German nursing sisters and two sailors on a sightseeing trip. The man nearest the camera, a Signalmaat, wears the gilt metal Narvik campaign armshield directly above his rate badge for that of signaller.

BELOW: Before the outbreak of the war and for the first year or so of the conflict the German naval practice of wearing ships' division strips continued to be worn. These can be seen on the upper right shoulder of two of the sailors in this photo.

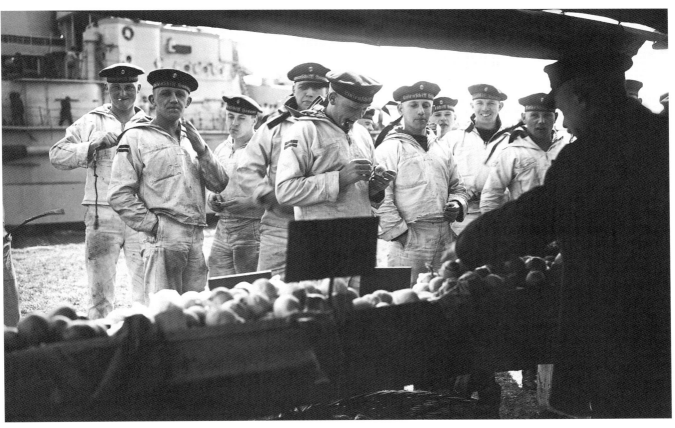

Naval Artillery

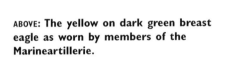

ABOVE: **The yellow on dark green breast eagle as worn by members of the Marineartillerie.**

Although the Third Reich's Kriegsmarine is usually associated with seagoing warships, it was also responsible for both the static and mobile coastal defence of Germany, and sometimes Nazi-occupied territories, as well as the related gunnery training, and it therefore developed a generally land-based sub-division known as the **Marineartillerie** (Naval Artillery) which was responsible for such military roles. Aside from any training activities its members were primarily tasked with manning batteries of various calibres to defend the German-held coast against Allied warships and aircraft and also fighting as ordinary ground troops if the need arose. Due to their unusual status within the Kriegsmarine members of the Marineartillerie were dressed in uniforms and wore insignia that were markedly different from those associated with their ship-based companions. Unlike sea-going personnel, from 1938 members of Marineartillerie regiments, along with NCO training battalions and later members of the Naval Air Spotting Company, were all issued with a uniform in field grey that closely resembled that issued to the Army as it was considered a more practical design for their specialist gunnery role. The most obvious difference between the Marineartillerie and other services was that gold-yellow was used in the design of their buttons, badges and so forth instead of the Army's and Navy's silver-white. However, there were also several other noteworthy variations in insignia.

The national/organisational emblem created for the Marineartillerie was also somewhat different from that worn by the sea-going personnel of the Kriegsmarine. It consisted of the traditional German national eagle looking to the right from the viewer's perspective and holding a wreathed swastika in its talons and, although the eagle had similar angular outstretched wings to the more common Kriegsmarine type, the overall badge design for the Marineartillerie was significantly less stylised in its appearance than that of its parent body with the bird of prey having much more realistically portrayed feet and feathers, for example. The Marineartillerie emblem, which measured approximately 10 cm at its greatest width and a little less than 5 cm deep, was rendered in gold-yellow thread on a field grey background to match the tunic and was worn above the tunic pocket on the wearer's right breast.

As with other formations, the Marineartillerie made use of shoulder straps, which were worn in matching pairs and featured emblems that were found in the wider Kriegsmarine. These generally consisted of a dark blue-green cloth on which was superimposed various other devices that indicated rank or groups of ranks and on occasion brief details of the wearer's unit or attachment. The most common device was an anchor, which was sometimes matched with a short piece of coiled rope, a design that echoed the buttons on the Marineartillerie tunic, or pairs of crossed anchors without the rope embellishment. Numerals and capital letters worn above the aforementioned devices might indicate individual units or attachments. The devices, of whatever type, were produced in gold-yellow thread, while various other additions such as bars, edgings and pips, either in silver-aluminium or gold-yellow, were used to indicate status. Marineartillerie personnel were also issued with collar patches, while the shoulder straps were worn in matching pairs. For ratings the patches comprised a dark blue-green background with Litzen, while for officers the device was similar, although the Litzen were generally larger and were produced with a mixture of silver-white and gold-yellow threads rather than grey-white and yellow.

Marineartillerie personnel were also permitted to wear both trade and speciality badges, but these tended to have a much more limited range than those available to their sea-going comrades and concentrated on the narrower body of skills required to serve and function within the coastal artillery, such as gunner and range-finder. As was common, the badges comprised a background colour to match the Army-inspired Marineartillerie uniform, which was field grey rather than the more usual dark blue-black and white of the wider Kriegsmarine, and they were generally oval or circular in design, measuring roughly 4–5 cm across and 7 cm (oval) high. Various devices were superimposed on these backgrounds to indicate proficiency and sometimes rank. These usually referred directly and clearly to the wearer's proficiency or trade by using generally recognisable symbols. For example, a driver was identified by a plain anchor over which appeared a steering wheel, while a secretary/writer was indicated by a pair of crossed quill pens. These designs were not necessarily unique to the Marineartillerie as they were usually identical or very close to those worn by similarly experienced Kriegsmarine personnel stationed on warships where there was an appropriate match. The various designs appeared in a range of colours, chiefly gold-yellow and red, and where relevant might also include chevrons in a matching colour to identify the wearer's rank, again a system followed elsewhere in the Kriegsmarine.

BELOW: **A member of a Marineartillerie unit with the rank of Obermaat.**

OPPOSITE: Men of a naval Flak battery load a shell into a heavy gun. The helmet bands being worn around the body of their steel helmets would indicate that this was an exercise.

LEFT: Troops from a Marineartillerie detachment receiving a visit from the commander-in-chief of German Coastal Artillery. Interestingly all the troops are wearing exercise helmet bands.

BELOW: The crew of a heavy coastal artillery gun seen during live firing practice.

OPPOSITE: **A member of an unnamed Marineartillerie unit observing through a scissors periscope.**

LEFT: **German prisoners taken during the Normandy campaign arriving at a British port from Cherbourg, 29 June 1944. Amongst the many captured troops were men of the Marineartillerie. It was their coastal positions that were the first to be overrun.**

BELOW: **An officer of the Marineartillerie taking a reading with the aid of a rangefinder. This heavy artillery unit took part in the siege of the Russian city of Leningrad.**

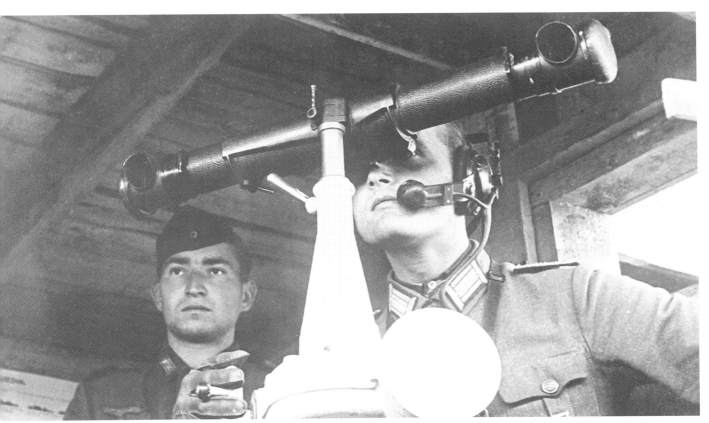

RIGHT: **With time on their hands the troops manning the prewar coastal artillery batteries would often use their spare time making toys for their children back home.**

BELOW: **A naval Flak unit searching the skies for Soviet aircraft. Every man stands ready at his station, the gun is camouflaged in scrim.**

OPPOSITE: **Troops of the Marineartillerie on the march.**

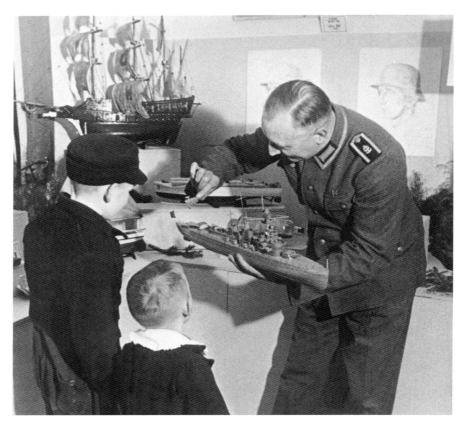

Allgemeine-SS

T he Allgemeine-SS (General-SS) was a vast organisation, some 240,000 men in 1939, which was effectively responsible for turning Hitler's political beliefs into reality. As a consequence its ranks were filled with the most dedicated Nazis. As such it was responsible for the administration of the Third Reich and was effectively a rival to other administrative bodies. Among its specific duties were policing, education and the resettlement of conquered territories in the east. The first SS units were established in 1925 and were chiefly responsible for the personal protection of Hitler. The organisation remained small for the remainder of the decade, and into the early 1930s was dwarfed by the SA under Ernst Röhm. The SS even wore uniforms that were similar to those of the SA and only varied in details such as black rather than brown kepis and black rather than brown ties. However, matters changed when Hitler ordered a purge of the SA in late June 1934, chiefly because it appeared to threaten both his position and undermine the further advancement of the Nazis. The instrument chosen to conduct the successful purge was the SS under Heinrich Himmler, who had been made Reichsführer-SS in 1929. Röhm and various other leading SA members were killed, creating a power vacuum that was filled by the SS with Hitler's full blessing.

The purge led to the SS gaining a separate identity and unchallenged position within the Nazi Party some four weeks later. This new status led to the introduction of revised dress regulations that remained basically unchanged until Germany's defeat. Single shoulder straps on the right shoulder were worn on the brown shirt (gradually replaced between 1933 and mid-1935), the replacement black uniform, and the similarly coloured greatcoat. The straps consisted of black material and various designs in silver-white thread were used to indicate various rank groupings. Reichsführer-SS Heinrich Himmler, head of the SS, wore a unique and complex design that comprised twisted cord and an oak leaf with acorns. Collar patches, worn in pairs and also revised in 1934, performed two functions – the left denoted rank, while the right displayed a device indicating the wearer's unit up to the the rank of Standartenführer. All patches consisted of a black background and various edgings and emblems rendered in silver-white thread. Rank identification included such devices as horizontal bars, pips and oak leaves with or without acorns. Unit designations on the right patch appeared in many guises – Arabic and Roman script, and graphic emblems, such as

OPPOSITE, ABOVE: **Members of an Allgemeine-SS signals unit stretch their legs on the platform of a railway station.**

OPPOSITE, BELOW: **Surrounded by senior party officials, ministers and uniformed members of the party machinery, Adolf Hitler greets German workers in the garden of the Reich Chancellery, Berlin, 1 May 1937, the Day of German Labour. Amongst the uniformed persons are members of the Allgemeine-SS.**

BELOW: **Men of the Allgemeine-SS receiving shooting instruction from an NCO of the Totenkopf Regiment.**

crossed lances and lightning bolts, for example. A lightning bolt, often appearing with a numeral, indicated membership of a particular unit's signals section, while crossed lances were used by mounted formations.

Cuff-titles, worn on the left arm, generally identified the wearer's unit or attachments to administrative bodies. They comprised a black band edged in a variety of colours – silver-white, red, green and blue, for example. Numerals in either Arabic or Roman script appeared with or without a unit name, while others often commemorated a Nazi Party hero involved in the failed Munich Beerhall Putsch of 1923 and were frequently rendered in Gothic lettering. Both the lettering and numerals appeared in silver-white. SS armbands, always worn on the upper left arm, developed out of those worn by the SA in the early days of the Nazi Party. The SA version had a red background and a black swastika imposed on a white circle edged with a narrow black line. From 1925 it was modified for the SS to include two black horizontal bands that ran slightly inside the top and bottom edges of the armband.

The Allgemeine-SS also made use of arm badges. These appeared on the lower left arm and were worn approximately one inch above any cuff-titles. They consisted of a vertical lozenge of black cloth and contained numerous devices in silver-white thread that were variously used to identify the wearer's attachment to a particular section or unit of the organisation, or his particular skill. The devices ranged from simple abbreviated lettering, or runes, through various German eagles and swastikas, sometimes with the addition of other symbols, to recognisable artefacts. 'SD', for example, standing for Sicherheitsdienst (Security Service), was worn by all SD members and the SS Main Security Office's staff, while the T rune denoted attachment to the SS's recruitment, procurement, and education department.

Long-standing members of the Nazi movement, including the Allgemeine-SS, were also permitted to wear badges to indicate their prolonged commitment to the cause. Those who could demonstrate membership of the party before 1933 were allowed to carry a chevron device on their upper right sleeve. The most common form consisted of three silver-white chevrons, which were either stitched directly on to the uniform or placed on a triangular black background and then attached.

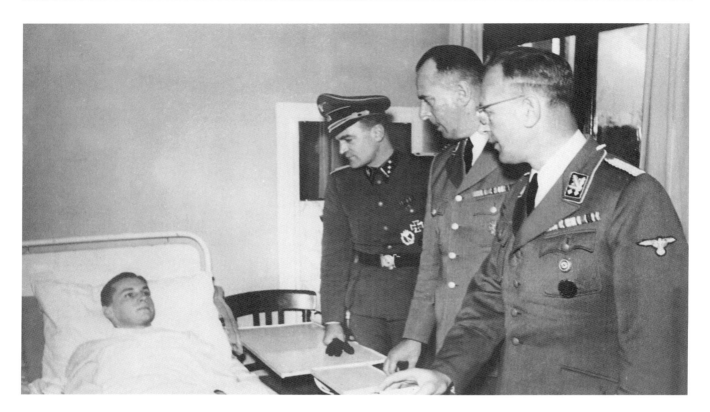

LEFT: Reich Commissioner for the Occupied Netherlands and Reich Minister without Portfolio Dr Seyss-Inquart talking to a wounded member of the Waffen-SS at a military hospital somewhere in the Netherlands, December 1942. Seyss-Inquart had been a prominent Austrian Nazi (Reichsstatthalter) and one of the founders of the Deutsch-Österreichischer Volksbund in Austria in 1938-39.

BELOW LEFT: Surrounded by black uniformed senior officers of the Allgemeine-SS, Hitler is greeted at Goslar by a delegation of mining officials. On the right of the picture is Staatsrat and SS-Gruppenführer Wilhelm Meinberg, Commissioner for Transport of Fuel on the board of the Four-Year-Plan and Manager of the Group 'Mining' in the 'Hermann Goering Werk'.

LEFT: The SS racing driver von Manstein seated behind the wheel of his BMW 328 coupe in which he won the Grand Premio di Brescia on 28 April 1940. The Grand Premio di Brescia replaced the Mille Miglia.

Certain items of sports clothing such as sports vests, shirts and shorts, fencing jackets and driving overalls frequently carried the motif of the wearer's branch of service or para-military service. Here is shown the regulation issue SS runes emblem, a 100 mm wide circular cloth badge.

BELOW: The Prince Regent of Yugoslavia, accompanied by Adolf Hitler together with Joachim von Ribbentrop (left) and Staatsminister Dr Meissner (right) slightly to their rear, pass through the main entrance of the new Reich Chancellery, Berlin, June 1939. The sentries in black uniform and white equipment presenting arms are members of the elite Leibstandarte-SS 'Adolf Hitler'.

OPPOSITE, ABOVE: **Celebrating Hitler's birthday – 20 April – in the 1930s. Standing in the garden of the Reich Chancellery and listening to the martial music from the band of 'Regiment List' are senior members of the state, the party and the military.**

From the right: Reichsminister Dr Goebbels; Ministerialdirektor and SS-Brigadeführer Dr Willy Meerwald, the deputy head of the Reich Chancery; Staatssekretär Dr Hans Heinrich Lammers, Chief of the Reich Chancery; Adolf Hitler; SA Stabschef Viktor Lutze and Hitler's military adjutant, Major Hossbach.

OPPOSITE, BELOW: **Arm in arm with General Karl Litzmann, Adolf Hitler accompanies the 85-year old German hero of World War I past the ranks of an SS Honour Guard drawn up from members of the Allgemeine-SS 'Adolf Hitler' Regiment.**

LEFT: **The Bavarian Minister of Culture, Gauleiter Hans Schemm, talking with the Treasurer for the Nazi Party SS-Oberstgruppenführer Xavier Franz Schwartz, wearing black uniform.**

Waffen-SS

The SS (**Schutzstaffel**, literally Protection Squadron) was established in 1925, with many of the first recruits coming from the ranks of the Freikorps, paramilitary groups of former World War I servicemen, and was a body steeped in Nazi ideology with its members owing absolute loyalty to Hitler. Ultimately a vast organisation, often described as a state within a state, under Heinrich Himmler it initially contained three chief military formations, the **SS-Verfügungstruppen** (SS–VT/SS reserve units), **SS-Totenkopfverbände** (SS Death's Head formations/concentration camp guards), and the **Leibstandarte Adolf Hitler** (Adolf Hitler's bodyguard), which were reorganised as the **Waffen-SS** in 1939. The Waffen-SS was comparatively small in its early days – in 1940 it totalled a mere 100,000 men as opposed to the German Army's 2.5 million – but gradually gained favour with Hitler, particularly after the Army had suffered the major defeat at Stalingrad in 1942–43, and subsequently underwent a dramatic expansion programme to include armoured, cavalry, infantry, motorised and mountain divisions. As it expanded, recruits came from several sources – German citizens, supposedly ethnic Germans living in other countries, and men from occupied Scandinavia and Western Europe. The net was eventually cast even wider as manpower shortages

BELOW: **Officers and men of the SS-Panzergrenadier Divisions Leibstandarte-SS 'Adolf Hitler', 'Das Reich' and 'Totenkopf' – all of whom had taken part in the recent fighting for Kharkov – being introduced to Dr Goebbels at his Berlin ministry.**

became apparent, with units being raised in Albania, Hungary, the Baltic States, the Ukraine and Yugoslavia. In total some 15 nationalities served in the Waffen-SS, around one million men in all.

The Waffen-SS divisions, which were often given preferential treatment in the allocation of new equipment, were regarded as ruthlessly efficient combat formations but the picture is more complex. The German, Western European and Scandinavian units were undoubtedly elite forces, but many of the other 39 divisions were of much poorer quality and several were dissolved in 1944. As the war turned against the Nazis, the Waffen-SS was increasingly used as a hard-hitting mobile reserve, rushing between threatened fronts to prevent Allied breakthroughs and launching localised counterattacks to stabilise the military situation. Gradually, however, the divisions were ground down, particularly on the Eastern Front, although many of the best units continued to fight on until the last days of the Third Reich. Despite their combat record, the renown of the Waffen-SS divisions was deeply sullied by numerous atrocities against both Allied soldiers and civilians in the occupied countries. Murders and massacres went hand in hand with the wholesale destruction of towns and villages, especially on the Eastern Front that for the Waffen-SS was first and foremost a racial and ideological war.

SS personnel did not wear the Nazi eagle and swastika badge on the right breast, but rather on the upper left arm at the midpoint between shoulder and elbow, and its design was significantly different from other organisational emblems. Appearing in white or light grey for enlisted men and silver for officers, it had pointed wings rather than the more standard clipped design and appeared on a black background. Shoulder straps and collar patches underwent modifications and it was not uncommon to find both being worn. From 1942, straps were black

BELOW: **Troops of the Waffen-SS undergoing training to become officers at the SS-Junkerschule Bad Tölz. This photograph was taken sometime during the war, as is evident from the various badges being worn, and the men were drawn from various units indicated by the 'Langemarck', 'Wiking' and 'Totenkopf' division cuff-titles.**

for enlisted men and edged in a branch of service colour (Waffenfarbe), the same as used by the Army. The addition of silver lace identified non-commissioned officers, while officers were denoted by either silver or gold braid placed on a background of the Waffenfarbe colour edged in black. Additional devices identified a particular rank and, on occasion, a particular unit. Collar patches were in the shape of a parallelogram, on a background of black cloth and worn in pairs. They were unpiped for enlisted men but had silver braid and/or pips for non-commissioned officers on the wearer's left collar. An officer's rank was also identified by the addition of various devices, such as pips and oak leaves, to the wearer's left collar. The right collar patch generally carried two silver SS runes to identify membership of the organisation. There were exceptions to this – many foreign Waffen-SS units employed other devices, but only the 3rd SS Panzer Division 'Totenkopf' of the ethnic German formations dispensed with the runes and employed the death's head motif.

Waffen SS troops sometimes dispensed with the usual system of rank designation when wearing certain types of uniform, including camouflaged snow suits, that did not use shoulder straps. Although ranks in the SS were named differently from those in the Army, the SS rank emblems followed those in use with the Army. They appeared on a black cloth background and comprised a number of bars, oak leaves and other devices in either green, yellow, or yellow and white. Better quality and finishes were reserved for more senior ranks, while those for personnel in junior ranks were usually silk-screened on to cotton.

Like other formations, members of the Waffen-SS with a long-standing affiliation to the Nazi Party and its various bodies were identified by length-of-service chevrons. These were generally awarded to individuals who had been full-

OPPOSITE, ABOVE: **The commander of the 7th Volunteer Mountain Division 'Prinz Eugen', SS-Brigadeführer and Generalmajor der Waffen-SS Arthur Phelps, directing officers on his staff. This unit's collar patch was the 'Odalrune' as worn by the officer in the foreground.**

BELOW: A scene during the fighting in Normandy, 1944. An officer of a Waffen-SS unit gives instructions to an SS-Mann. The officer wears a camouflage jacket that appears to be manufactured from Italian Army camouflage material as the patterning is not of the standard issue Waffen-SS type. The officer wears on his left arm the green and black printed cloth badge for his rank of SS-Sturmbannführer.

BELOW LEFT: The black on white armband 'In Service of the Armed SS' worn by uniformed and civilian persons working with the Waffen-SS.

BELOW: The distinctive cornflower collar patch peculiar to the 22nd Volunteer Cavalry Division of the SS 'Maria Theresa'.

time and active members of the party before Hitler became German chancellor in January 1933. In the case of the SS the chevron was worn on the right arm, halfway between elbow and shoulder, and consisted of a black background with three narrow silver-white chevrons. In 1935 individuals in the SS who had been associated with either the armed forces or police before Hitler's assumption of power were further identified by the addition of a central pip to the original design.

Many of the Waffen-SS divisions were awarded cuff-titles, which were worn on the lower left sleeve. These consisted of a black cloth band edged with silver braid and, usually, the unit's name in Gothic or Roman script in white, light grey or silver. Some also carried the SS runes. In some cases individual regiments were permitted to wear cuff-titles. For example, the three combat regiments of 2nd SS Panzer Division 'Das Reich' – 'Germania', 'Deutschland' and 'Der Führer' – each had name titles.

The Waffen-SS also made use of arm badges which were worn on the left forearm above any cuff-title. These consisted of various emblems, runes, and lettering in silver-white on a black lozenge-shaped background and could variously identify such things as rank, function, or trade. In addition some emblems were worn on the upper right arm, such as the black cloth oval with the Edelweiss used to identify SS troops trained in mountain warfare.

ABOVE: **A youthful member of the SS-Freiwilligen-Legion Niederland. The 'Wolf Hook' worn on the right-hand collar patch was the emblem used by this Dutch Waffen-SS volunteer legion.**

RIGHT: **Members of a Waffen-SS war correspondent unit picking olives somewhere in the south of France. The SS-Unteroffizier nearest the camera is wearing their distinctive German script cuff-title.**

OPPOSITE, ABOVE: **A gunnery officer from the SS-Standarte 'Germania' range-taking from within a bunker of a heavy coastal artillery emplacement. The right-hand collar patch with the double runes and the number '2' indicates his regiment. This officer would have been wearing the 'Germania' cuff-title on his left forearm, not shown in this photograph.**

OPPOSITE, BELOW LEFT: **A member of the 7. SS-Freiwilligen-Gebirgs-Division (Volunteer Mountain Division) 'Prinz Eugen' operating in the Bosnian mountains examining the contents of a case containing signal flares. The 'Odalrune' collar patch device identified members of this unit.**

OPPOSITE, BELOW RIGHT: **This SS-Mann is the unit signaller as evinced by the trade badge on his lower left sleeve.**

OPPOSITE, ABOVE: **Members of 17th SS-Panzergrenadier Division 'Götz von Berlichingen' squat in line as prisoners of war under the watchful eye of their US captors waiting to be transported to a prisoner of war camp, July 1944.**

OPPOSITE, BELOW: **One million, three hundred thousand telephone calls in 220 days. This switchboard operator from the Totenkopf Regiment was one of a team of field operators who were capable of transmitting this vast amount of telephone traffic.**

LEFT: **An SS-Sturmmann standing at the 'present arms' position.**

ABOVE: The use of SS runes on both collar patches was a feature of the early SS-Verfügungstruppen units. Shown here is one Dr Lardschneider, his cheek marked with duelling scars, wearing not the standard twin runes' collar patches but the unusual combination of a mirror pair of runes patches, is an indication that insignia errors were created in the early development stages of the SS-VT and Waffen-SS.

ABOVE RIGHT: A routine security check on the papers of an infantry soldier. A member of the SS Feldgendarmerie closely scrutinises the documents.

LEFT: SS signals women. This photograph was taken of the first SS women to be seen in public wearing the new style field grey uniforms introduced for these SS-Helferinnen.

RIGHT: Somewhere in southern Russia two men of the Waffen-SS carry jerry cans filled with water as well as water bottles strung on a pole. Both men wear tropical helmets, shorts and sports vests with the SS sports symbol.

SS-Polizei-Division

Frundsberg

Reinhard Heydrich

Götz von Berlichingen

Horst Wessel

Florian Geyer

Hohenstaufen

Frundsberg

Reichsführer-SS

Adolf Hitler

Adolf Hitler

Adolf Hitler

Adolf Hitler

Germania

Germania

Das Reich

Der Führer

Deutschland

Deutschland

Wallonien

Fallschirmjäger

SS Kavallerie Division

SS-Feldgendarmerie

SS-Kriegsberichter

SS-Kriegsberichter-Kp.

Adolf Hitler

OPPOSITE: A range of SS cuff-titles, most of which are self-explanatory. The first five in the left-hand column (SS-Polizei to Horst Wessel) are BeVo quality cuff-titles. At the bottom of that column are variations on the SS-Leibstandarte Adolf Hitler cuff-title. The right-hand column shows more cuff-titles including variations (German Gothic and ordinary script) of those for the 'Germania' and 'Deutschland' divisions. At the bottom of that column are variations of the cuff-titles worn by members of the SS-Kriegsberichter Kompanie (SS-War Reporter company) and another Leibstandarte cuff-title.

LEFT: SS-Hauptscharführer Hubert Walter wearing service dress with breeches with a Leibstandarte 'Adolf Hitler' cuff-title.

BELOW: A tunic being examined by British field intelligence somewhere in Normandy, 1944. The cuff-title 'Adolf Hitler' together with the prewar, third-pattern shoulder strap with its distinctive pointed end indicate that it belonged to an SS-Unterscharführer

Foreign Volunteers

OPPOSITE AND BELOW: Three examples of BeVo-manufactured arm shields for wear by non-German foreign volunteers.

OPPOSITE, BELOW: Introduced after July 1944, this shield was worn by east European troops, many of them Russians, serving in the 1st and 5th Regiments of the Don Cossack Division. The letters B and A are in fact Cyrillic letters equivalent to our V and D standing for Voysko Donskoye. The red and blue were the traditional colours of the Don Cossacks.

BELOW: The arm shield worn by members of the Spanish Blue Division.

Although Hitler's wars were campaigns of conquest and each victory invariably heralded an occupation characterised by oppression and brutality, the Wehrmacht was able to attract hundreds of thousands of foreign volunteers to its ranks, probably around 1.5 million in total, with most being drawn from Eastern Europe, particularly the western provinces of the Soviet Union and the Baltic States. The foreign recruits and units that fought to expand or defend the Third Reich did so for two main reasons – personal commitment to Nazi ideology or a desire to create an independent homeland free of foreign domination or colonial rule. Nazi propaganda often portrayed the Wehrmacht as a liberating force dedicated to the destruction of communism and also railed against the iniquities of colonial rule, and both were messages that appealed to many people in Eastern Europe and beyond. In retrospect it is clear that the propaganda masked the true reality that the Nazis would never accept any new political orders other than those that were wholly under their absolute control, but many at the time failed to recognise the fact and accepted the message at face value. Equally, the German armed forces became short of manpower as the war continued and Nazi racial policies were somewhat relaxed to allow those previously regarded as 'inferior' peoples to fight. Many foreign volunteers served in combat and were only withdrawn after suffering severe losses, but others carried out supporting roles in the rear, such as anti-partisan operations to free German troops for front-line combat. Many who survived the war received short shrift from the victors, especially Stalin, who ordered their imprisonment or execution.

Generally, those recruits from Western Europe, both occupied and unoccupied, joined up because of their support for Nazism, while those from Eastern Europe and farther afield served Hitler in the cause of their own nationalist beliefs, particularly people from states recently liberated by the Third Reich but previously ruled by the Soviet Union. Many of these last were former members of the Red Army, recruited while living under usually dreadful conditions in German prisoner-of-war camps but equally fearful of what any future liberation by the Soviet Union might bring to both themselves and their families. Some volunteers joined on their own initiative and served with like-minded countrymen once inducted, others followed the lead of the organisation to which they belonged and joined en masse, and some, such as those who formed the 18,000-strong Spanish Division Azul (Blue Division), answered an official call for volunteers from their own government and arrived as a fully-formed unit. Finally, some European states were effectively ordered by the Nazis to 'donate' armed forces to the struggle. Many volunteer units had two designations. For example, the

Blue Division was more formally known as the German Army's 250th Infantry Division while the Legion Volontaire Français contre la Bolshévisme (Anti-Bolshevik French Volunteer Legion) was more manageable when retitled as the 638th Infantry Regiment (France).

The majority of foreign volunteers acted as ground troops, attached either to the Heer (Army) or Waffen-SS, although some were supplied to the Kriegsmarine and Luftwaffe, and served in most theatres of war. They were either integrated into a particular German unit or fought as an independent command, although sometimes under German officers. The independent commands varied in strength but could be anything from a battalion to a division, although Lieutenant-General Andrei Vlasov, a former Soviet Army commander captured in 1942, led the large but short-lived Russkaia Osvoboditelnaia Armiia (Russian Liberation Army) formed in November 1944. In contrast, other volunteer units were so small – little more than company strength – that they had little use other than propaganda value and were used to depict Germany's war effort as an international crusade.

In general, volunteer personnel were kitted out in exactly the same way as any other German soldier with the standard uniform and equipment but some, particularly already established units from nominally independent countries such as Croatia and Slovakia, might wear items of clothing or uniforms that indicated their background. Original badges of rank and medals were also sometimes worn. Cossack cavalry units wore traditional headdress, while Sikh members of the nationalist Azad Hind Fauj (Free Indian Legion) continued to use the turban. Croatian and Slovakian troops wore khaki uniforms of local design rather than the German field grey equivalent.

The most common form of badge to identify Hitler's foreign volunteers was an emblem, usually shield-shaped, worn on either the upper left or right arm, roughly midway between elbow and shoulder. These were produced in a number of ways and materials and are found finished to different standards, although the majority were silk-screen printed. These devices came in a variety of designs and colours but clearly denoted the background or allegiance of the wearer. Colours and the emblems sometimes imposed on them reflected the wearer's nationality. Croatian volunteers were identified by a red-and-white chequerboard badge borrowed from the official arms of Croatia, while the badge of the Free Indian Legion incorporated three horizontal stripes in yellow, white and green, colours that had been adopted by the pro-independence Indian National Congress. The badge of the Russian Liberation Army was based on the pre-communist colours of the red, white and blue imperial flag and included the czarist St Andrew's cross. Other heraldic symbols were occasionally superimposed on these backgrounds. The black-edged deep yellow badge worn by Flemish recruits from Belgium included a rampant lion, the traditional emblem of Flanders, in black with its claws and tongue picked out in red. The third element in the emblem design was common to most and consisted of script, either letters or, more frequently, a single word. 'Wallonie', 'Georgien', 'Latvija', all typical examples, clearly identified the wearer's origins, while letters were abbreviations of a unit's designation. The latter were most commonly used by volunteer units from Eastern Europe and often consisted of Cyrillic script. The Russian Liberation Army's patch included the Cyrillic letters POA while Ukrainian volunteers had a badge using YBB standing for the Cyrillic rendition of the Ukrainian Liberation Army.

ABOVE: **The arm shield for members of the Terek Cossacks in the Cossack Cavalry Corps and introduced for wear after July 1944. The black and cornflower blue quartered arm shield worn on the left upper arm were the traditional colours of the Terek Cossacks. The white letters T B were the Cyrillic letters equivalent to the Latin letters T V – Tereskoye Voysko.**

RIGHT: **A Dutch volunteer, serving in the Waffen-SS with the rank of SS-Sturmmann. He wears in the button hole of his tunic the ribbon of the Iron Cross 2nd Class together with the Eastern Front medal. On his left breast pocket he wears his NSB (NS Beweging – the Dutch Nazi Party) badge, a small triangular badge pinned to the pocket immediately above the infantry general assault badge, which in turn is next to the wound badge in black metal. On his shoulder straps he wears black cloth slip-ons displaying the capital letter 'R', probably in red stitching.**

ABOVE: **The Latvian arm shield. This particular item was manufactured in Riga. The shield displayed the national colours of Latvia – dark red, white, dark red – which were the colours of the Latvian national flag.**

RIGHT: **A dog handler preparing food for the guard dogs operating with the Latvian Legion. The arm shield, slightly different in design to that featured above, is shown being worn on the handler's right upper arm. Although this was not unusual, the correct position of wear for this arm shield was on the left upper arm.**

ABOVE LEFT: The arm shield intended to be worn by Hungarian troops serving in the German Army. No pictorial or written evidence exists to prove that this item was actually worn and it is believed that, although the shield was manufactured by BeVo of Wuppertal as can be seen from the small black lettering across the material at the base of the badge, it was never actually used.

ABOVE: Joseph Goebbels, Reich Minister for Public Enlightenment and Propaganda and Gauleiter of Berlin, greeting selected members of the German Army and Waffen-SS at his Ministerial Offices in Berlin. The soldier he is shaking hands with is a member of the Croat Legion, as indicated by the man's arm shield.

LEFT: The Croat Legion arm shield. The red and white checkerboard design was taken from the arms of Croatia. The red lettered 'Hrvatska' is the Croatian spelling for Croatia.

LEFT: Troops of the Armenian Legion were identified by the arm shield show here. The chosen colours of red, blue and yellow were the colours of the flag used by the short-lived Independent Armenian Republic that existed from 1918 to 1921.

BELOW: SS-Untersturmführer Gerades Mooymann, one of the first 'Germanic' volunteers in the Waffen-SS. At the age of 20, as an SS-Sturmmann and gunner serving in the 14th Anti-Tank Company of the SS-Freiwilligen-Legion 'Niederland', he destroyed 15 Soviet tanks. For this action on 20 February 1943 he was awarded the Knight's Cross of the Iron Cross. He was the first non-German to receive this award. For propaganda purposes the bestowal of his Knight's Cross presented the Propaganda Ministry with the golden opportunity for Mooymann to be held back from rejoining his regiment. Instead, arrangements were made for him to make a number of personal appearances in Holland and the Low Countries. He is shown on one of these occasions surrounded by members of the Dutch NSB and being interviewed by a Waffen-SS war correspondent.

LEFT: **A bugler of the Free Arab Legion.**

BELOW: **The arm shield worn by troops from the Caucasian region of the Soviet Union. This is the second design arm shield with the title 'Bergkaukasien' (Caucasus Mountains) in yellow across the top edge of a blue field displaying three yellow horse heads conjoined to a circle in a rotating form.**

BELOW LEFT: **The BeVo quality arm shield worn by troops serving in the Georgian Legion.**

LEFT: An SS-Hauptsturmführer of the Brigade d'Assault 'Wallonie'. This officer wears, on his left upper arm, the Walloon arm shield displaying the Belgian national colours of black, yellow and red.

RIGHT: The original pattern arm shield worn on the left upper arm by members of the Flemish NSKK Transport Brigade (NSKK Transportbrigade Flandern). In July 1943 these Flemish volunteers were merged with other French, Dutch and Walloon NSKK volunteers to form the NSKK Transportgruppe 'Luftwaffe', and their Lion of Flanders arm shield was withdrawn and replaced by the Wolf's Hook emblem, a black rune on a yellow, sometimes orange, shield.

BELOW: Members of the Flemish Volunteer Legion (Freiwilligen Legion 'Flandern') accompanied by their wives at an indoor meeting, believed to be in Brussels. The two uniformed soldiers nearest the camera are both wearing the Black Lion of Flanders arm shield on their left forearm.

ASERBAIDSCHAN

LEFT: **A member of the Dutch Volunteer Legion putting the finishing touches to a model dolls house. The shield worn on his left cuff directly above his unit cuff-title, 'Frw. Legion Niederland', is divided diagonally into the three colours – orange, white and blue – the original national colours of the Netherlands dating from 1574. The Dutch national colours of red, white and blue that were officially introduced in 1796 also featured on these Dutch Legion arm shields as there were at least four patterns of arm shields in use at various times.**

BELOW LEFT: **One of the arm shields worn by volunteers from Azerbaijan. This was the unit's first pattern arm shield that was in use during 1942-43. The tribar of blue over red over green were the national colours of the Azerbaijan region of the then Soviet Union.**

OPPOSITE, ABOVE LEFT: **The arm shield of the Ukrainian Liberation Army. The Cyrillic letters that appear as 'YBB' stand for Ukrainske Vyzvolne Viysko.**

OPPOSITE, ABOVE RIGHT: **The arm shield worn by members of the Russian Liberation Army. The Cyrillic letters that appear as 'POA' stand for Russkaia Osvoboditelnaia Armiia. The motif of a blue saltire on a white shield – the opposite of the Scottish saltire – was chosen as this was the emblem of St Andrew, the patron saint of both Russia and of Scotland.**

OPPOSITE, BELOW: **Five members, supposedly five brothers, of the 13th Waffen-Gebirgs-Division der SS 'Handschar' (Kroatische Nr.1). Originally this mountain division was known as the Croat SS Volunteer Division, and some time later as the Croat SS Volunteer Mountain Division. In October 1943 the title changed when it was appointed to bear the number '13' becoming the 13th Frei. Gebirgs Division (Kroatien). Its final title as above included the word 'Handschar'. This is Turkish for a scimitar, a symbol that, combined with a swastika, was used on the collar patches worn by the troops of this division.**

 As the majority of the personnel of this division were Moslems they were permitted to wear a green or a red fez complete with SS eagle and death's head.

Sturmabteilung

ABOVE: A member of the Berlin SA searching through the fire-damaged contents of a fish shop. The cuff-title he wears was one awarded to those SA units distinguished by bearing the names of German or Nazi heroes. The wording in light grey cotton on a black band was in German script and spelt out Hans E. Maikowski. It was worn by members of Standarte 1 from Group Berlin-Brandenburg.

Formed in 1921 the **Sturmabteilung** (SA/Storm Detachment) was one of the earliest components of the Nazi Party and performed two functions – the protection of officials and those attending mass meetings, and the suppression of rival political activists through street fighting and intimidation. Many of the original recruits had been World War I veterans and had served with the postwar right-wing Freikorps, paramilitary bodies used to fight left-wingers and otherwise 'maintain order' in Germany, before switching to the SA. The organisation was originally headed by Captain Pfeiffer von Salomon but in January 1931 Ernst Röhm was made its chief, overseeing the SA's expansion, reorganising it along military lines, and outfitting members in the brown shirts that gave them their nickname. By 1932 the SA had a membership of 400,000 and was chiefly engaged in smashing the German Communist Party, the main rival to the Nazis.

Hitler initially envisaged the SA as the spearhead of a violent revolution that would bring the Nazis to power and gave full backing to its campaign of intimidation but in 1933, against a backdrop of growing street violence, the SA was banned by the then German president, Paul von Hindenburg. Hitler agreed to the decision, fearing that its activities might undermine his attempt to win power through the ballot box rather than violent revolution. The SA appeared firmly wedded to the latter idea and also proposed a socialist-style state but Röhm also argued that his organisation should be integrated into the Army and eventually supplant its traditionalist leadership. His plans were opposed by the generals, and Hitler, moving away from his earlier socialist programme towards a policy of ardent nationalism, wanted to curry favour with the military establishment and moved to suppress the organisation. When he became chancellor in 1933, Röhm continued to argue his case and Hitler made the decision to bring the SA to heel by purging its leadership, which appeared to be preparing a coup. Variously known as the Blood or Röhm Purge or the Night of the Long Knives, the decapitation of the SA occurred in late June 1934 – some 180 leading Nazis, including Röhm, were killed, but by no means all were members of the SA. The SA was reorganised in 1935 but its pivotal role within the Nazi Party was conceded to the SS, which had carried out the purge.

From the early days of the Nazi Party, SA members generally wore the standard Nazi swastika armband in red, white and black on the upper left arm between elbow and shoulder, although there were variations, often relating to a particular branch or assignment. The SA Sports Association, for example, wore an armband with a red background, and white circle on to which had been superimposed a wreathed swastika and sword in copper. The SA also made use of cuff-titles, which were introduced from 1933 and consisted of a 30–33 mm wide band. Generally there were two categories – those worn on the left forearm by groups of ranks belonging to the various SA staff guards and those worn on the right forearm by the more general membership. The former, which were modified in 1934, came in various colours corresponding to the wearer's collar patches with a range of edgings and lettering in diverse colours. For the wider SA, cuff-titles often highlighted figures considered important or significant to the Nazis. These bands consisted of a black background embellished with the names of those being commemorated in a range of scripts embroidered in silver-white thread.

Early SA uniforms were rudimentary with many being identified by the wearing of little more than the standard Nazi Party swastika armband and an unstandardised brown shirt, but from 1927 more elaborate insignia began to appear, initially just collar patches. The first full dress regulations appeared in 1933 but these were subsequently modified in 1938 and these later regulations remained in force until 1945. For ranks up to Standartenführer, the right-hand patch identified rank and the left the wearer's unit; above the Standartenführer grade both patches denoted rank. Initially only a single shoulder strap was worn on the right shoulder but after 1938 they were worn in pairs. In the case of the earliest shoulder straps and collar patches variously coloured material was used to identify the wearer's SA district of service. For example, members from the Thüringen (Thuringia) district were identified by a vibrant light green. Coloured threading was also added to shoulder straps to denote groups of ranks, while collar patches had various devices to identify similar groups. Unit designations and various emblems to denote branch of service were added to the patches from 1931.

The SA also made use of arm badges denoting rank, trade and proficiency, and most were worn on the lower left arm. These came in a variety of shapes – oval, triangular and square, for example – and had several different background colours. Superimposed on the background cloth were numerous devices, including runes, artefacts, symbols and letters, that also appeared in coloured threads, such as silver-white, red, and yellow. As was common, signallers had a lightning bolt

BELOW: The armband for wear by SA-Reserve II members whose ages were between 35 and 45 years. Whilst it was a standard swastika armband it had the addition of one-centimetre-wide flat, silver-grey braiding either stitched to – or in some cases woven into – the band as an integral feature, along the top and bottom edges of the band. The band was worn on the upper left arm. This band ceased to be used after 1935 when the SA-Reserve II was incorporated into the regular SA.

RIGHT: **A party of SA men about to set out on a cross-country ski run. The SA man taking a compass bearing and holding up a map is wearing the SA cuff-title embroidered with the honour name of Rudolf Erlbacher. This indicates that he was a member of Standarte 9 from SA Group Südmark. The officer nearest the camera wears the Tyr rune emblem on his left shoulder. This red, white and black badge was worn by those persons who had successfully passed through the National Leaders School (Reichsführerschule).**

BELOW: **Chief of Staff of the SA Viktor Lutze shown here in full regalia and wearing his SA honour dagger. He also sports a Tyr rune above his swastika armband.**

device, while a qualified dentist (Zahnarzt) could be identified by the letter Z in Gothic script.

The SA employed two means of identifying the wearer's length of service: chevrons and rings. So-called Alte Kämpfer (Old Fighters), members who had joined the Nazis prior to Hitler becoming chancellor in 1933, were identified by a chevron device on the upper right arm. The background colour was brown if the chevrons were not stitched directly onto the item of clothing and the chevrons comprised three gold-yellow and two red upright Vs. Uniquely, the SA also denoted length of service prior to the end of 1933 by combinations of rings of varying thicknesses, usually 4 or 12 mm wide, in grey-white, worn on both cuffs of jackets, shirts, and greatcoats. Various combinations were worn, but generally the more rings worn by the individual the greater the length of service, and there was no distinction in style, colour, or finish quality between ranks. As examples, anyone who had served with the SA during 1925 was entitled to wear two 12 mm and two 4 mm rings, while membership in 1933 was indicated by a single 4 mm ring.

LEFT: **The third and final pattern of the SA sports emblem – the SA-Brustwappen – was a comparatively large badge with a diameter of approximately 137 mm. It featured the SA motif worked on a disc of white cloth and employed the relevant SA group's colours. It was normally worn on the front of the vest, the motif being the same for all SA districts, the colour and the initial letters showing the SA district. This one was worn by SA Group Warthe and the colour used was described as cornflower blue.**

BELOW: **SA-Obergruppenführer Wilhelm Schepmann, the last SA Chief of Staff, salutes General von Bock. The sleeve rings around the tops of Schepmann's tunic cuffs indicate his length of service prior to February 1933. The two 12 mm wide and two 4 mm wide silver-grey sleeve rings on each forearm showed that he first enrolled as a member between 1 January and 31 December 1925, and qualified as an 'Alte Garde', an Old Guard.**

FAR LEFT AND ABOVE: A selection of first pattern SA shoulder straps that were in use between 1933 and 1938. These were worn singly, on the right shoulder of the Brownshirt uniform and the officer's tunic and later the SA greatcoat. The coloured underlay to these straps indicated the wearer's SA district, each district having been allocated a colour.

LEFT: A member of the elite SA-Standarte 'Feldherrnhalle'. The purge of the SA leadership – the Night of the Long Knives – took place on 30 June 1934. This resulted in the formation of a new elite SA guard unit designated 'Feldherrnhalle' in honour of the monument in Munich where the National Socialist Putsch of November 1923 was ended. The new SA guard units were garrisoned in Berlin, Munich, Stettin, Stuttgart, Hattingen and Krefeld with an extra Sturmbann raised and stationed in Vienna after the Anschluss in 1938. The particular mission of the SA-Standarte 'Feldherrnhalle' was the guarding of NSDAP offices, especially those in Berlin and Munich. Members of this Standarte wore the regulation pattern SA uniform. Their collar patches, shoulder strap underlay and kepi top were carmine red in colour. They wore a 'Feldherrnhalle' cuff-title and when on guard duty and for parades they wore a special gorget (Ringkragen).

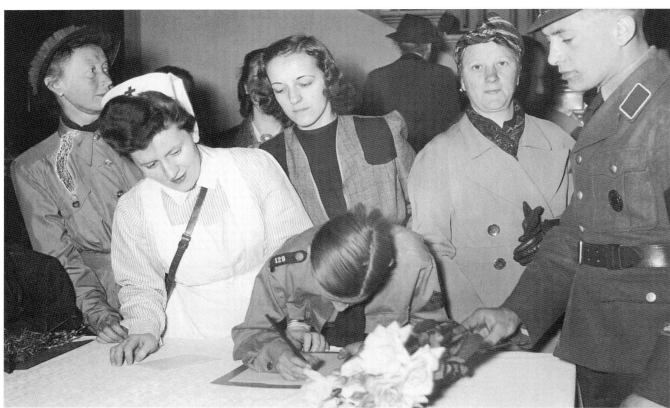

LEFT: **Motorised patrols for German motorways and major roads started on 1 April 1935. Here an officer of the SA-Feldjägerkorps sits at the wheel of a police car alongside an official of the Protection Police. The colour chosen for use by the SA Police for its kepi and collar patches was white, the only SA formation to use this colour.**

BELOW LEFT: **Ernst Röhm, SA Chief of Staff.**

BELOW RIGHT: **Viktor Lutze succeeded Röhm.**

OPPOSITE, ABOVE: **Viktor Lutze at a Christmas display held in Berlin. He is surrounded by onlookers and officers and men from the SA-Standarte 'Feldherrnhalle'.**

OPPOSITE, BELOW: **A Deutsches Jungvolk member signs his name to a greetings document to Hitler on his 54th birthday. He is watched by a German Red Cross nurse and by a member of the SA-Standarte 'Feldherrnhalle'.**

ABOVE: **A propaganda portrait of what the SA saw as a typical Brownshirt member. The shape of the SA national emblem, the small metal eagle and swastika badge with its narrow pointed wing feathers worn on the front of the kepi, indicates that this is an early period photograph. The 'crushed' shape of the kepi was a feature of these early street fighters and is emphasised by the way he wears his chin strap under his chin. Although this is a black and white photograph, it is most likely that the kepi top and collar patches are black indicating that he was from the SA district Berlin-Brandenburg.**

ABOVE RIGHT: **The German Olympic champion Rudolf Harbig photographed standing next to the Reichssportsführer von Tschammer und Osten.**

RIGHT: **The 'Standortführer Gross-Berlin' armband being distributed to members of the SA-Standarte 'Horst Wessel' who are to act as police auxiliaries, 13 November 1933.**

LEFT: **First pattern SA shoulder straps for wear by SA officers from 1933 to 1938 (except, as captioned below). Note that the colour of the strap identified the district – thus black was used for Berlin-Brandenburg and for Niederrhein, sulphur yellow for Franken and Schlesien, etc. From top to bottom:**

The first strap was worn by officers from SA-Oberführer to SA-Obergruppenführer.

The next strap was worn by the ranks of SA-Sturmbannführer to SA-Standartenführer from 1939 onwards.

The next two straps are the earlier version of the last, worn 1933–38 by SA-Sturmbannführer to SA-Standartenführer. Both are on sulphur yellow backgrounds but in this case there is a differentiation between Franken (gold braiding) and Schlesien (silver braiding).

The final four straps were worn by officers from SA-Sturmführer to SA-Sturmhauptführer. Apple green was the colour appointed to be used by SA districts of Thüringen (gold braiding) and Sachsen (silver braiding).

RIGHT: **Final pattern shoulder straps for wear by SA other ranks. These straps were introduced during the period 1938–39 and continued to be used until the end of the war in Europe. All the straps shown here were for wear by the lowest SA ranks of SA-Sturmmann to SA-Haupttruppführer. The underlay colours instead of indicating the wearer's SA district as had been the case with the previous pattern straps now reflected the wearer's branch of SA service. Pale grey was used for all SA foot units, including the SA-Standarte 'Feldherrnhalle'. Bright red was for those assigned to SA headquarters, dark blue for medical units, black for SA engineers, green for Jäger troops, lemon yellow for signals and orange yellow for SA cavalry units.**

Veterans' Organisations

BELOW: **A comparatively early photograph taken of Hauptmann Ernst Röhm, the Chief of Staff of the SA, the SS and the Steel Helmets (Stahlhelm). He is greeting the German Crown Prince Wilhelm of Prussia at the gathering of 60,000 members of the Stahlhelm organisation held in Hanover on 24 September 1933. Standing between Röhm and 'Little Willy' is the Bundesführer of the Stahlhelm, Minister Franz Seldte.**

From the end of World War I until Hitler's assumption of power in 1933, several independent, highly nationalistic, right-wing organisations of 1914–18 ex-servicemen were involved on the fringes of the country's political life. Many became associated with the Nazis during their early struggles in the 1920s and were later brought under their direct control. Chief among these was the **Stahlhelm** (Steel Helmet) organisation, which was formed in 1918 by two officers, Franz Seldte and Theodor Duesterberg, and incorporated into the **NS-Reichskriegerbund** (NS-RKB/National Socialist League of Ex-Servicemen) from March 1938. The ex-servicemen's leagues all wore some form of military dress and insignia indicating rank and branch of service on formal or public occasions.

Rank and service branch were indicated by cloth collar patches, while oval or shield-shaped badges worn on the upper right arm of the Stahlhelm field grey tunic

by all ranks indicated the district to which the wearer belonged. Twenty-five are known to have existed and each came with an heraldic emblem usually associated with a particular Land (state) or city. From 1938, NS-RKB members were identified by new black cuff-titles that reflected the former league's reorganisation. These indicated a member's affiliation to one of the 18 new administrative areas and his official position. Ordinary members, for example, had a simple black cuff-title with grey cotton edging, the administrative area named in Gothic script and flanked by crossed swords. Senior leaders had similar designs but with gold-coloured metallic thread, while staff had the designs picked out in silver-white.

The most important heraldic legacies of the early leagues were associated with the Brigade Ehrhardt and first seen during its involvement in the failed Kapp Putsch in Berlin during 1920. Created by ex-naval officer Hermann Ehrhardt, the unit was based on the No. 2 Naval Brigade, a Freikorps body identified by the swastika often painted on its members' helmets, which had ousted a socialist administration in Munich the year before. The black cuff-title worn on the left forearm of the brigade's uniform incorporated the SS runes emblem that was later adopted by the Nazi Party for its own Schutzstaffel.

RIGHT: A veteran member of the German East African colonial troops. Dressed in the uniform worn during World War I this old soldier wears the Southern Cross emblem on his left forearm.

Nazi Party Political Leadership

The **Nationalsozialistische Deutsche Arbeiterpartei** (NSDAP/NS German Workers' Party) grew out of the Munich-based Deutsche Arbeiterpartei, which was founded in 1919 amid the unrest that followed Germany's defeat in World War I. Although the party was small it gained a new recruit in September 1919, former soldier Adolf Hitler, who quickly proved not only a dynamic, rabble-rousing speaker but also an able administrator who revitalised the group's structure and attracted increasingly large audiences to its events. In 1920 the DAP changed its name to the NSDAP and founded the Sturmabteilung (SA/Storm Detachment) to maintain order at meetings which had often been disrupted by left-wing activists. A year later Hitler manipulated an internal crisis in the NSDAP, forcing the party to accept him as its sole leader. Against a background of growing unrest in Bavaria, chiefly due to activities of radical socialists, Hitler decided to launch a coup attempt in November 1923 believing that the 70,000-strong NSDAP was powerful enough to challenge both the radicals and the legitimate administration. The so-called Beerhall Putsch proved to be a gross mis-reading of the political situation and was easily suppressed by the authorities, leaving the NSDAP in disarray; Hitler was imprisoned during 1924 but the following year announced a new Nazi Party. Despite opposition from some long-standing supporters, Hitler abandoned many of the party's old radical policies, which had alienated the more

BELOW: A delegation of Spanish officials received in Berlin, 30 December 1942. The Governor of Madrid and Provincial Chief of the Spanish Falangists, Carlos Ruiz-Garcia, is seen in conversation with the German Military Attaché to Spain, Graf Rocca-Mora.

LEFT: **The fourth and final pattern of collar patches worn by political leaders from 1938 to 1945 displayed not only the wearer's rank but also his level of political responsibility. This was achieved, in the case of the latter, by the use of distinguishing colours and in the former by a series of pips, braided bars or oak leaves displayed on the patches. (See also the patches on page 110.) Shown here are a pair of collar patches for a political leader with the rank of Obergemeinschaftsleiter within the political level of the Ortsgruppe – indicated by blue piping on light brown patches.**

BELOW: **A pair of collar patches for the rank of Hauptgemeinschaftsleiter within the political leadership level of the Kreisleitung.**

OPPOSITE TOP: **The 1935 Reich Party Day gathering at Nuremberg. The great hall appears to be packed with most of the prominent members of the Nazi party. In the front of the picture from left to right are: Gauleiter of Franconia Julius Streicher; Adolf Hitler; Reichsminister and Deputy Führer Rudolf Hess, holding the honour sword of the City of Nuremberg; SA-Obergruppenführer and Oberbürgermeister of Nuremburg Willy Liebel; Reich and Prussian Minister for Ecclesiastical Affairs SA-Obergruppenführer Hans Kerrl; Reichsminister for Public Enlightenment and Propaganda Dr Paul Joseph Goebbels, Reich Propaganda Chief of the NSDAP; Reichsminister of the Interior Dr Wilhelm Frick; and Reichsminister without portfolio Dr Hans Frank, President of the Academy of German Law.**

Others that can be identified are – from the left and in the second row – Reichsminister Robert Ley, Chief Party Organisation Manager and Leader of the German Labour Front; Reichsführer-SS Heinrich Himmler; and directly behind them, Reichsleiter Alfred Rosenberg; Joachim von Ribbentrop, Reich Minister for Foreign Affairs; SS-Obergruppenführer Karl Wolff, Personal ADC to Himmler; Konstantin Hierle, Reich Minister of the Reich Labour Service; Walter Darré, Reich Minister for Food and Agriculture; Otto Dietrich, Reich Press Chief of the NSDAP; Albert Speer, then Hitler's personal architect; SS-Obergruppenführer Karl Demelhuber; and Minister of War General Werner von Blomberg,

OPPOSITE, BELOW: **An armband for a Leiter eines Hauptamtes (leader of a high office) in a Kreisleitung. When worn correctly – on the left upper arm – the line of golden oak leaves swept upwards**

RIGHT: **The ubiquitous party armband, an essential item of dress for members of the Nationalsozialistische Deutsche Arbeiterpartei – the Nazi Party. It was worn on the left upper arm. Its quality depended on the budget of the wearer. The item shown has a unit stamp that authorised its issue.**

conservative sections of German society, opted to pursue power through the ballot box, and set about turning the Nazis into a national force in German political life by imposing a rigid and disciplined structure on its members. Evidence of the party's discipline and new direction was revealed at the first, superbly stage-managed, Nuremberg rally in 1927, which was organised to promote the Nazi political programme and reveal its 'respectable' face to a wider audience.

Hitler's new direction gradually attracted adherents to the party, which had a membership of 178,000 by 1929, but a major breakthrough on the national stage seemingly eluded the Nazis – they had won just 12 seats in the 1928 elections. Salvation came with the Great Depression, which brought mass unemployment and political turmoil. The disillusioned lower middle classes, which were suffering severely, were attracted by the Nazi Party's radical proposals to solve the crisis and deal with the often violent political unrest. Many turned to Hitler in the 1930 election. The Nazis won 107 seats, making them the second largest party in the Reichstag (German parliament), but the traditional establishment – conservative politicians, industrialists, and the armed forces command – remained wary of Hitler. The 100,000-strong paramilitary SA, for example, was viewed by many conservatives in Weimar Germany's Reichswehr (armed forces) as a threat to their own status.

In 1932 Hitler attempted to challenge for the leadership of Germany but on both occasions lost to the sitting president, the aged Paul von Hindenburg. However, in July the national elections saw the Nazis gain seats in the Reichstag and one of their leaders, Hermann Goering, was made president of the parliament by his peers. Thirty-seven percent of the popular vote had given the Nazis 230 representatives in the Reichstag but no overall majority, yet Hitler, with the mobilised SA at his back, demanded the chancellorship from Hindenburg. The state president refused to bow to Hitler's demands and in the November elections the Nazis suffered a backlash, their Reichstag presence dropping to 196 seats.

ABOVE: **Collar patches for, from left to right: Abschnittleiter (section leader) at Ortsgruppe level (the latter indicated by the pale blue piping); Hauptabschnittleiter (senior section leader) at Kreis level; and at Gau level the badge of an Obergemeinschaftsleiter (senior community leader). See also the patches on page 107.**

OPPOSITE, ABOVE: **Sports vest emblem for members of the Auslander organisation**

OPPOSITE, BELOW: **A delegation of German colonists from South and Central America arriving at Frankfurt am Main is seen here being greeted by Gauamtsleiter Hellerman of the Auslander organisation. On his right is Landesgruppenleiter Arnold Margerie and on his left Dalldorf.**

Even so Hitler, as the leader of a major force in a country rent by instability and fractured politics, could not be ignored by the conservative political establishment, who believed that he and his party could be controlled and used against the left-wing radicals which they saw as the greater threat. In January 1933 they offered, and Hitler accepted, the position of chancellor in a new coalition cabinet, but only three Nazis were given ministries. The new cabinet proved unworkable and Hitler, making capital out of a situation he had partly engineered, called for a further round of elections. Evidence of left-wing plans for revolution and a fire at the Reichstag in February, masterminded by the Nazis but blamed on the radicals, convinced many to support or acquiesce in a decision to suspend civil liberties and arrest thousands of left-wing activists. In March the elections duly took place, although with socialists and communists banned from the Reichstag, and the Nazis gained 288 seats with 44 percent of the vote. This was not an overall majority but, with the aid of 52 other nationalists, Hitler had the support he needed to remould Germany and create the Third Reich through the wide-ranging process termed Gleichschaltung (co-ordination or unification), a sweeping, top to bottom transformation of Germany and its people along National Socialist lines. The Nazi Party was already a large and disciplined organisation and, in its years of struggle, had effectively created a state within a state. From 1933, as part of Gleichschaltung, this parallel administration and its numerous sub-divisions were welded onto or superseded the old institutions that had overseen Germany's pre-Nazi era affairs.

As befitted a diverse and highly bureaucratic organisation, the Nazi Party had numerous levels of political leadership, stretching downward from Hitler to the party activists responsible for a residential block. Perhaps the most obvious sign of party membership was the swastika armband in red, white and black, and the party's political leadership made full use of the symbol. Armbands based on the basic design were worn on the upper left sleeve, with various parallel bands in white to indicate rank in the earliest versions. The system was somewhat haphazard and was regularised during 1938–39. This proved a vast undertaking due to the complexity of the Nazis' political leadership structure. Some 38 individual bands were designed to indicate rank and branch or area of responsibility. Various designs were added to the basic armband, principally bars and oak leaves that appeared in various sizes, combinations and positions. Edgings in various colours were also included to identify the wearer's membership of one of the four basic divisions of the political leadership (see below for details).

Rank was usually denoted by combinations of shoulder straps (mostly dropped in 1934) and collar patches, and these underwent various changes – four in all during the period from 1933 to 1938, when the final revisions were instituted. The first pattern, which was instituted in 1933 and remained in place until 1934, was relatively simple, reflecting the still-incomplete rank and grading system the Nazis had before they achieved power. However, a new pattern was introduced in 1934 that was based on three territorial grades and one for general leadership responsibilities and these distinctions became the basis for subsequent developments. In the former case there were three distinct levels – Gau (district), Kreis (circuit), and Ortsgruppe (local group) – and all groups were served by leaders of various ranks. Generally, membership of a particular responsibility group was indicated by a facing colour, while from 1934 rank was denoted by various additions to the basic design of the collar patches. These included, for example, chevrons, traditional Litzen, variously coloured edgings, oak leaves, pips, wreaths and the Nazi eagle and swastika emblem in silver-white or gold-yellow.

RIGHT: The Alte Kämpfer Winkel – the Old Fighters' chevron – was worn by those who had been members of the Nazi Party before the NSDAP gained political power (30 January 1933).

OPPOSITE, ABOVE: Amidst the bomab and fire-damaged buildings, Gauleiter Grohé of Köln (Cologne)–Aachen addresses a mass gathering, July 1943.

OPPOSITE, BELOW: A simple, printed armband for a member of the Nazi Party Readiness Squad (NSDAP-Partei Bereitschaft.

BELOW: Deputy Führer Hess greets German students – some wearing national costume – on the 15th anniversary of the formation of the NS Students Group. This gathering took place in the Führerhaus in Munich on 27 January 1941.

By the time of the final set of changes in 1938, the NSDAP's political leadership had become so complex that there were within the four territorial and general leadership groupings a staggering 97 separate ranks: 27 relating to the Gau level; 22 to the Kreis; 17 to the Ortsgruppe; and 28 to the general. To these must also be added three special insignia that, for example, related to other groups such as retired political leaders. Through necessity the original four colours of light and dark brown, light red, and carmine were expanded to include other hues such as dark blue and black and a series of edging colours was introduced giving the following grouping identification – Gau dark red edging on a bright red background; Kreis white on dark brown; Ortsgruppe light blue on light brown; and general gold-yellow on carmine.

Cuff-titles were also worn. At the most basic they might be nothing more than a means of identifying the wearer's date of membership of the party or commemorating one of its early organisations or branches. Most common of these were bands worn on the lower left arm by both students and teachers attached to Nazi Party political leadership schools (Ordensburgen). These generally comprised a brown background with a title in gold-yellow Gothic script that might be the name of a particular school or the more general title 'Ordensburgen'. The NSDAP political leadership also made use of various arm badges, generally on the upper or lower left arm. Generally, they gave some indication of rank or branch of service, although others also indicated date of entry into the Nazi Party until these were abolished and replaced by the above-mentioned cuff-title. The badges varied in style but most comprised a lozenge-shaped background patch in black within which appeared various identifying letters, symbols or party-related insignia such as the eagle and swastika.

ABOVE: A delegation of German officials arriving in Madrid, March 1943. This picture shows, from left to right: The German Ambassador von Moltke; SS-Obergruppenführer Lorenz, in the greatcoat; Landesgruppenleiter der NSDAP Tessmann and the Cultural Attaché at the German Embassy Dr Petersen, wearing civilian dress and holding his hat. Interestingly Political Leader Tessmann is wearing the Luftwaffe Flak War Badge instituted on 10 January 1941 and awarded to those persons who had manned heavy and/or light gun batteries and searchlight batteries and who had successfully destroyed a certain number of enemy aircraft.

LEFT: Visitors to the 1941 Viennese Autumn Fair. Reichsleiter Baldur von Schirach (hands on hips) together with the Reich Finance Minister Graf Schwerin von Krosigk in dark uniform together with Generalmajor von Schell admire a wood gas generator.

OPPOSITE: Another view (see also page 8) of the VIPs at the German gymnastic and sports festival at Breslau in July 1938. In addition to the senior people in front there are a number of police, political, Allgemeine-SS and German Red Cross uniforms among the spectators.

Political Education Schools

BELOW: **Young boys from one of the prewar National Political Education Schools enthusiastically brushing down their uniforms in the open air. These lads, all of whom are below the age of 14, wore a uniform almost identical to that worn by members of the Deutsches Jungvolk. However, they were distinguished as Jungmänner by displaying on their single narrow, flat black shoulder strap (right shoulder) the white embroidered letters NPEA and wearing a sleeve triangle on their upper left arm bearing the letters NPEA above the location of the school. Those shown here appear to be from National Political Education School at Schulpforta near Naumburg (Saale).**

One of the Nazis' central policies on gaining power was to create a highly motivated and politically reliable cadre of supporters to run and maintain the Third Reich effectively. Political education was central to this policy and the leadership established a network of specialist elite schools both within and outside Germany in which enrolment was based on age. Those young Germans deemed to have attained the entrance requirements first joined the NPEA (**Nationalpolitische Erziehungsanstalten** – National Political Education Schools) from the age of ten. The development of the NPEA, which were commonly referred to as Napolas, began shortly after Hitler came to power. The original three were founded on 20 April 1933 – Hitler's birthday – and the network grew to a total of 42 by 1944. Two were also established in occupied Holland and one in Belgium and these were known as **Reichsschulen** (Reich Schools). Above the NPEA were two other types of school – the **Ordensburgen** (Castle Schools) attended by those aged between 24 and 27 and the **Hohe Schule** (High Schools) of the Nazi Party, which took students in their late 20s and early 30s.

The Napolas had a determinedly military ethos that drew inspiration from the prestigious cadet colleges formerly associated with Germany's imperial past. Nazi students, like their predecessors, were expected to show a suitably martial spirit and the school curriculum included drills, marches, and field exercises. Rather than being termed forms or classes, groups of students, who were formally addressed by the title of Jungmänner, were known as platoons. Aside from the physical side of the programme, pupils studied a wide range of topics based on Nazi educational principles.

NPEA uniforms were generally plain and carried only little embellishment. Field grey tunics might be paired with brown or black trousers for both students and their teachers. Narrow shoulder straps often bore the letters NPEA in Gothic scripts, while various other combinations of devices were used to denote rank within the organisation. As was the usual practice, armbands consisting of the standard red white and black swastika, but appearing in various designs, were worn on the upper left arm. From the early part of the war the Napolas became more and more closely associated with the SS and this was reflected in the clothing worn by the students. Along with the wearing of Waffen-SS-style uniforms, that body's eagle and swastika organisational emblem was adopted. As with members of the SS, students took to wearing the symbols on their upper left arm midway between elbow and shoulder.

NS Motor Corps

The **Nationalsozialistisches Kraftfahrer-Korps** (NSKK/NS Motor Corps) was an integral part of the Nazi Party and a paramilitary transport organisation which was initially a branch of the SA. However, following the purge of the SA in 1934, it gained a separate identity and received new insignia to reflect its independent status. It subsequently became closely involved in training recruits for the Army's armoured and motorised formations. During World War II the NSKK was co-opted into supporting the Wehrmacht by supplementing Army and Luftwaffe transport formations and its various units were formed into regiments or brigades and, from 1944, a dedicated military transport corps.

The NSKK organisational emblem was somewhat distinct from the standard national device and comprised a modified eagle with clearly reworked wings above which was positioned a scroll bearing the letters NSKK. It was fixed to the upper right arm, and the eagle and motto appeared in silver-white on a background cloth that matched the colour of the wearer's uniform. As was common, collar patches identified the wearer's rank and unit. Rank appeared on the left hand patch, while the unit designation was found on the right patch. The overwhelming majority of patches had a black background, although occasionally red was used. Superimposed on the unit patch were various abbreviations, letters, numerals and short words, usually in silver-white thread, to identify a particular formation. Shoulder straps, mostly worn singly on the right shoulder, although members of wartime-raised units might wear two, comprised a black background with usually silver-white thread to indicate one of six rank groupings and a piping colour to indicate a particular unit, subdivision, or location. Some more senior ranks had both silver-white and gold thread or other devices, such as an oak leaf with acorns.

Arm badges were generally worn on the left or right forearm depending on their nature and appeared in a range of designs. Most comprised black backgrounds shaped as ovals, triangles, rectangles and lozenges superimposed on which were numerous devices in usually silver-white or white thread, although gold-yellow was sometimes used. The emblems consisted of runes, letters, swastika-based devices and so forth, and commonly identified the wearer's branch of service or status. All ranks of the NSKK were entitled to wear the usual swastika armband on their upper left arm but there were variations that replaced the Nazi eagle and swastika with the previously described NSKK organisational emblem. Other armbands were also worn when NSKK personnel were undertaking specific duties such as traffic control, although they were only worn for the duration of the task in hand.

NSKK units also wore cuff-titles on occasion. These had several functions and might identify a particular formation, commemorate a leading Nazi figure, or be presented to an individual as an indication of a honorary position. Generally, they

ABOVE: **Three versions of the National Socialist Motor Corps eagle and swastika national emblem. The top one was worn on the right upper arm of the light brown shirt or tunic. The central one, slightly smaller than the arm eagle, was worn on the front of the black NSKK kepi. The lower eagle was worn on the right upper arm of the olive green NSKK greatcoat. Approximately a year or so before the outbreak of war the position for the arm eagle was altered so that, in place of the swastika armband, these eagle emblems were worn on the left arm, even though the eagle's head faced to the rear of the wearer.**

RIGHT: **NSKK shoulder straps, in keeping with the system used by members of the SA, did not represent individual ranks but rather each pattern represented a small range of ranks. The first three straps illustrated here were worn by NSKK ranks from NSKK-Sturmführer to NSKK-Sturmhauptführer, whilst the lower two straps were those for a NSKK-Staffelführer to a NSKK-Standartenführer.**

The underlay to these and other NSKK straps was black but the edging was finished with a narrow strand of Russia braid stitched around the edge. This braid was in a colour that indicated the wearer's NSKK unit, in the same manner as the prewar SA shoulder strap underlay colours indicated the SA district. The prewar colours displayed on these NSKK straps are, from top to bottom: black for Motor-Brigade Berlin-Brandenburg and for Motor-Brigade Niederrhein; dark brown for Motor-Brigade Westmark; orange-yellow for Motor-Brigade Südwest and Motor-Brigade Mitte; and finally, light blue for Motor-Brigade Hochland and Motor-Brigade Bayerische Ostmark.

BELOW: **NSKK shoulder straps for lower ranks.**

had a black background with silver-white edging top and bottom between which would appear the relevant names and lettering in Arabic or Gothic script in matching colours. Long-standing members of the organisation were also permitted to wear length of service chevrons on their right upper arms. They comprised a background material matching the particular uniform colour, the chevrons themselves, and an integral NSKK organisational badge. Colours for the emblem varied from silver-white to gold-yellow.

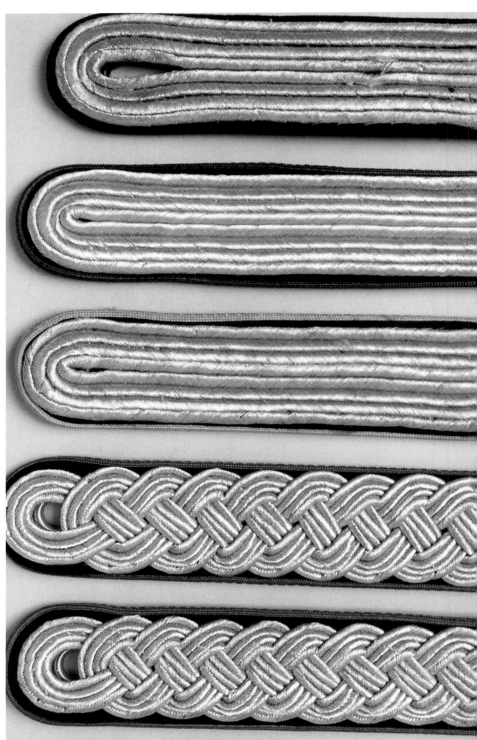

LEFT: **Two examples of the NSKK motor driver's diamond (Kraftfahrraute). Initially this badge was worn by all NSKK members on the left forearm of their shirt, tunic, motoring coat and greatcoat. By 1939 its use was restricted to those officers and men who held a vehicle driving licence, and thus it became a true badge of qualification. The left-hand diamond is of the first type, having the early pattern eagle and swastika emblem in pressed white metal set on a wheel with eight visible spokes all mounted onto a black cloth diamond. The right-hand diamond has the second pattern eagle a swastika and a wheel showing only six spokes, machine embroidered in silver-grey threads on a background of black silk.**

BELOW LEFT: **The right-hand collar patch and cuff-title of the 1st NSKK Transport-Regiment 'Luftwaffe'. The design of the collar patch is in the stylised form of the letters S and P standing for 'Speer'. These were worn by officers of the NSKK transport brigades and regiments in mirror pairs.**

BOTTOM LEFT: **A pair and two single badges as worn on the left side of the NSKK side cap. The background colour corresponded with the wearer's shoulder strap branch colour.**

BELOW **The NSKK sports vest emblem.**

NS Flying Corps

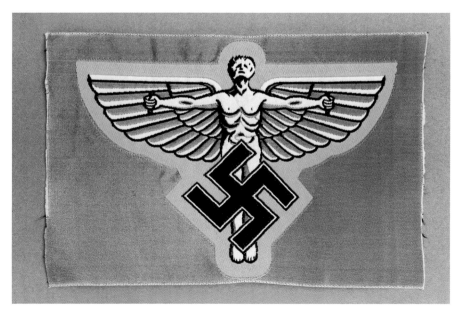

ABOVE: The NSFK national emblem as worn on the blue-grey uniform.

BOTTOM: The NSFK emblem of the quality for wear on sports vests and track suits.

Although Germany had been prohibited from developing an air force after World War I under the provisions of the Treaty of Versailles, the military leadership of the Weimar Republic, chiefly head of the Reichswehr General Hans von Seeckt, ordered the creation of supposedly civilian air sports clubs which offered members the opportunity to develop their flying skills on gliders or civil aircraft which were not wholly prohibited by the treaty. The **Deutscher Luftsport-Verband** (DLV/German Air Sports League) was formed under Bruno Lörzer in 1933 to promote flying further by bringing the previously separate groups together under a single organisational umbrella and this was subsequently superseded in 1937 by the **NS Flieger-Korps** (NSFK/NS Flying Corps), a body of mainly instructors initially headed by General der Flieger Friedrich Christiansen. Both the DLV and the NSFK were the sources for the skilled aircrew and trained pilots who formed the backbone of the Luftwaffe, the existence of which was officially announced to a stunned international community by Hitler in March 1935. At this stage its strength totalled some 1,900 aircraft and 20,000 personnel.

Membership of the DLV was shown by an organisational symbol carried on the upper left sleeve consisting of a grey-blue oval incorporating an eagle holding a wreathed black swastika in its talons. The eagle and wreath came in various colours to denote seniority – grey-white for lower ranks, silver-white for officers, and gold-yellow for senior ranks. A similar design formed the basis for the DLV armband worn on the upper left sleeve. DLV collar patches worn in pairs, and shoulder straps, first worn singly on the right and later in pairs for some grades, became the basis for those worn by the Luftwaffe. Collar patches had a coloured background indicating branch of service – gold-yellow for flying personnel, for example – with various additions and various combinations of edgings, stylised wings, bars, oak leaves and wreaths in either silver-white or gold-yellow to denote seniority. Shoulder straps consisted of a number of designs, including a grey-blue background with a light blue edging for lower ranks and various combinations of edging, and silver-white and gold-yellow cording for higher ranks.

The DLV also used various trade and proficiency badges. The latter were worn on either the left (sometimes right) breast and comprised three main types – on a grey-blue background silver-grey wings incorporating a black swastika, or various oval designs incorporating edgings, worn by pilots and radio operators; bird-like designs in similar colour combinations that denoted various levels of experience gained with the DLV's Abteilung-Segelflug (Glider Section); and combinations of balloon, wreath, eagle, swastika and the lettering DLV to denote balloon training. Trainers in the glider section had various lozenge-shaped breast insignia to denote rank. Various other trade badges were also worn by DLV personnel up to and including non-commissioned ranks on the left forearm and comprised appropriate, often symbolic, designs in silver-white on a grey-blue oval background.

The NSFK uniform and insignia were authorised in 1937 and many of the latter bore a close resemblance to those of the Luftwaffe, particularly the grey-blue (colour of the Air Force uniform) and yellow (the branch of service colour used by Luftwaffe fliers) used in many of the NSFK's emblems. The organisational badge, found on either the breast or arm, comprised the image of a gold-yellow winged man outlined in black, probably modelled on the Greek legendary character Icarus, onto which was superimposed the Nazi swastika in black outlined in gold. The background cloth matched either the grey-blue material of the NSFK's uniform jacket or the tan brown of the formation's work shirt. Shoulder straps, worn only on the right before World War II but on both shoulders during the conflict, were designed for groups of ranks. They grew in complexity from the simple grey-blue edged gold-yellow design for lower grades to gold-yellow-edged styles incorporating silver-white or gold-yellow cording for the various senior groupings. NSFK collar patches, worn in pairs throughout its existence, carried details of the wearer's unit on the right up to the rank of NSFK-Obersturmbannführer and rank on the left. The rank patches consisted of grey-blue cloth with yellow edging for all ranks, although senior ranks' versions (worn in pairs above Obersturmbannführer) had additional silver-white cording and various devices – bars, pips, oak leaves, wreaths and the organisational symbol – to denote their status. Unit details on the left-hand patch comprised numerals, letters and abbreviations.

The NSFK also instituted a range of proficiency and trade badges for its personnel and these consisted of various designs in white on grey-blue cloth circles or ovals and were worn on the left breast or forearm respectively. As with other branches of the Nazi regime, long-standing members of the NSFK were also permitted to wear length of service chevrons on the upper right arm; the silver-white chevron was backed on either grey-blue or tan brown cloth to match the uniform or shirt colour.

ABOVE: **Collar patches and shoulder straps as worn within the NSFK. The background colour of the collar patches and the cloth of the shoulder strap was the same as the blue-grey of the NSFK uniform. The colour yellow was the corps' appointed colour. This was used as piping around the collar patches, piping to the lower rank shoulder straps and underlay to the shoulder straps of their officers.**

The left-hand patch is that of an NSFK-Obergruppenführer, the right-hand patch for wear by an NSFK-Sturmmann. The upper shoulder strap was worn by officers from NSFK-Sturmbannführer to NSFK-Standartenführer, the next by personnel from NSFK-Sturmführer to NSFK-Hauptsturmführer, and the lower strap was worn by an NSFK-Anwärter to those with the rank of NSFK-Obertruppführer.

LEFT: **An official portrait of the Inspector of the NSFK-Obergruppenführer von Bülow. He wears the 'flying man' emblem above his right breast pocket and the second pattern national emblem on the upper edge to the front of his kepi.**

State Labour Service

The **Freiwilligerarbeitsdienst** (FAD/Volunteer Labour Service) and **Reichsarbeitsdienst** (RAD/State Labour Service) were part of Hitler's drive to reduce Germany's cripplingly high unemployment levels in the 1930s by requiring work from all able-bodied German males aged between 19 and 25 on either a voluntary or compulsory basis. The imposition of a strict regime on the young workers was also seen as a countermeasure to their sometimes supposedly disruptive social behaviour that was anathema to the Nazis and a means of instilling in them a suitable degree of discipline that would prepare them for compulsory military service, which was introduced by decree in 1935. Work with the FAD was voluntary state service, but a law announced on 26 June 1935 made it obligatory for all men to work under RAD direction, mostly in agriculture or on public works, such as the developing motorway network. Women were subsequently included in the programme within the sub-division of the organisation known as **Reichsarbeitsdienst der weiblichen Jugend** (RADwJ/ Young Women's State Labour Service) and were mostly employed in domestic or other supposedly traditional roles deemed appropriate by the Nazi hierarchy. Those required to serve were inducted on a yearly basis and the first draft totalled some 200,000 males, who were subsequently divided into two equal groups, with each serving for six months. The state-sponsored scheme was seemingly successful – in 1936 Hitler was able to announce that the labour service system, along with other measures, had reduced unemployment from six million in early 1933 to around one million. The head of the RAD was Reichsarbeitsführer Konstantin Hierl, who controlled the RAD's national bureaucracy and oversaw the work of its district and local sub-sections.

The RAD's organisational insignia comprised a swastika set on a representation of a vertical shovel blade placed between two ears of wheat. Colours for the cloth version worn on the cap were white for the wheat ears and shovel with the black swastika set within a red border mirroring the shape of the shovel's blade. The organisational symbol was also carried on the upper left sleeve as an armband and came in a range of forms, some including the device surrounded by an eagle and wreath. The standard swastika armband was also worn, while RAD personnel co-opted to serve alongside the Wehrmacht during World War II frequently wore a simple band that included the words 'Deutsche Wehrmacht' to indicate their status. Rank was denoted both by shoulder straps and collar patches, both of which were generally worn in matching pairs, and underwent several revisions between 1936 and 1942. When RAD staff were on active service they might wear fatigues and, in these circumstances, rank was displayed on the upper left arm in a range of chevrons, hollow triangles and pips.

RAD personnel also made extensive use of cuff-titles worn on the left arm. Many simply indicated the regional department to which the wearer belonged (state, north, south and so on), while others provided more detailed information, perhaps indicating a particular Gau (administrative district) and the RAD group's or section's designation. The titles came in a variety of styles and colours, sometimes including hues that had some relationship to the particular district of origin. Generally, gold-yellow lettering and numerals were reserved for the most senior positions within RAD, silver-white identified membership of a particular group or officers, while white lettering and numerals were used to indicate personnel belong to a particular section, usually lower ranks. Background colours were usually either black or brown, although various other colour combinations were found, and lettering was either Roman or Arabic, with the latter being reserved for lower ranks.

One of the most ubiquitous insignia worn by RAD members was the Dienststellenabzeichen (service position badge) that appeared on all types of uniforms and greatcoats. They were worn on the upper left arm and gave details of the wearer's unit or detachment and a broad indication of rank. All of the badges consisted of a shovel on either a black or brown shield background but there were colour distinctions relating to the central shovel motif to distinguish between groups of ranks – white was reserved for lower grades and silver-white for higher positions. Various forms of lettering and numbers, generally picked out in red on the shovel, indicated a particular RAD unit, training school or national administrative section.

RAD members also carried a range of other insignia on the sleeves of their uniforms. There was the Funktionszeichen (branch of service badge) that was manufactured in two types, again reflecting rank. Both consisted of motifs on a shield-shaped background. These were machine-woven in white thread for lower ranks and in silver-white for higher grades. Motifs often reflected the branch of service. For example, members of the RAD legal department were identified by a sword and scales and musicians by a lyre.

OPPOSITE, ABOVE: The RAD spade emblem was a distinctive feature of Reich Labour Corps uniforms. By the use of numbers and letters it was the means whereby RAD unit designations were displayed. Colour played a minor part in these arm shields, the most obvious use being the colour of the spade. The complete badge was produced machine-woven in either silver threads, for officers – and frequently in white cotton, for other ranks – or gold threads for the Reichsarbeitsführer and members of his staff with the rank of Generalarbeitsführer and above. The badge shown here – introduced in December 1935, with the red, capital letter 'M' on a silver spade – was worn by communications officials with the rank of either Hauptmeldbeamter or Meldbeamter.

OPPOSITE, BELOW: The RAD officer in the centre foreground is wearing the spade badge with the red letter 'M' as described above. The occasion for this open-air gathering was the mass burial of the victims of an air raid on the town of Saargemund in October 1943.

LEFT AND BELOW: A single and a pair of shoulder straps as worn by Volunteer Labour Service personnel. These, and other items of insignia including collar patches, were the first pattern items of Labour Corps insignia introduced in 1936.

ABOVE: A member of 811 Section of RAD Abteilung 275.

ABOVE RIGHT: First, the arm spade badge worn by an officer of the 4th Section of Labour Battalion 177. Then the badge worn by an officer staff member of a Reich Labour Service unit for female workers, in this instance Bezirk XX.

RIGHT: The Reichsarbeitsdienst sports vest emblem. The red, white and black were the German national colours and the spade or shovel head combined with the twin wheat ears were a fitting symbol for this labour organisation.

ABOVE AND ABOVE LEFT: **Three more RAD arm badges. From left to right: first, one for another rank of the 7th Section of RAD Abteilung 353. Next, the badge worn by an officer on the staff of an RAD Arbeitsgau, in this instance the Labour Region XXXI based on Karlsruhe. Interestingly this was the only Arbeitsgau out of a total of 40 such regions that was not specifically attributed. Its original headquarters were in Cologne (Köln). Its name bore the prefix 'W' (not displayed on the arm shield) and the unit was intended to be the nucleus around which RAD work groups from all parts of the Reich employed by the Wehrmacht on the construction of the Westwall, also known as the Siegfried Line, were to form. Finally, the badge displaying the red Gothic letter 'W' – believed to stand for 'Wehrmacht' or possibly 'Westwall'. This arm badge was the original pattern worn by officers on the staff assigned to the headquarters of the original Arbeitsgau XXXI.**

LEFT: **An example of the unit badge worn on the upper left sleeve of the tunic and greatcoat by all members of the RADwJ (Reichsarbeitsdienst der weiblichen Jugend), the female section of the Reich Labour Service. The Roman numeral shown below the RADwJ emblem indicated the wearer's district or RADwJ Bezirk number.**

RIGHT: As with a number of German political and paramilitary formations the insignia used to indicate rank was frequently changed. It was not unknown for rank insignia to undergo four complete changes resulting in four sets of insignia, all being worn within the space of the 12 years during which the Nazi Party was in power. This was the case with the Reich Labour Service. They underwent three changes, introduced at different times. The first pattern insignia, both collar patches and shoulder straps, were brought into use in 1936; the second in 1940; and the last and final introduction in 1942. All the collar patches shown here are of the third and last pattern. The patch with pale blue backing was worn by an RAD-Oberfeldmeister of the Justice Department.

RIGHT: Collar patches from two separate issues of insignia. The left-hand item, two individual patches and not a pair, were of the second pattern for the rank of RAD-Unterfeldmeister. The right-hand pair are of the first pattern and were worn by an RAD-Obervormann.

ABOVE: **Cuff-titles were worn within the RAD. Emsland was a commemorative title worn on the left forearm of the service tunic and greatcoat by those who had originally served in the pre-1933 Freiwilligerarbeitsdienst in the area of Germany centred around the River Ems.**

The Armelstreifen, which displayed a single Gothic script capital letter, was a feature of cuff-titles issued to those engaged in construction work on the Siegfried Line. They were introduced in January 1939 and withdrawn, or at least ceased to be issued, from the end of April 1941. The cuff-title with the letter 'S' is known to have been worn by RAD workers in the Saar area. As with the spade badges, these cuff-titles were produced with their capital letters and solid 5 mm deep and 60 mm long bars in white cotton threads for other ranks, silver-aluminium for officers and gold for senior officers.

RIGHT: **RAD collar patches of the second pattern, introduced in 1940, showing four separate ranks.**

German Labour Front

The **Deutsches Arbeitsfront** (DAF/German Labour Front), headed by Dr Robert Ley, was the only trade union tolerated by the Nazi leadership. It was established in early 1933, when detachments of the SA invaded the offices of the various existing independent labour organisations and seized their assets at the precise moment Hitler was pledging to bring stability to industrial relations during a May Day speech. The leadership of the unions was purged and their affairs were henceforth run by members of the Nazi Party under the umbrella of the DAF. Matters such as contracts and wage levels were set by officials known as Trustees of Labour, the chiefs of 13 regional departments across Germany. The take-over effectively ended union independence – the workers lost many rights with the DAF administrators also making deductions for income tax, insurance, union membership and periodic deductions instigated by the regime in time of crisis. However, the great reduction in unemployment engineered by the Nazis in the 1930s due to rearmament and public works, down from 5.4 million in June 1933 to around one million by spring 1937, was sufficient for many workers to accept the loss. All workers had to carry a log book recording their employment history and could not find a new position without producing it for inspection by a prospective employer.

The DAF organisational insignia consisted of a cog wheel encircling the Nazi swastika, but was generally only displayed on uniforms as a metal badge or pressed into waist belt buckles. Collar patches were not used but the shoulder straps worn in pairs by uniformed DAF members consisted of a black background, with variously coloured edgings and, for senior grades, the addition of the organisation's cog wheel emblem in either gilt or silver-white metal. Insignia for the 12 ranks of the DAF were also worn on the upper right arm. These consisted of a system of bars and chevrons in different numbers, with the latter also varying in design with some grades having a 'twisted' appearance. Backgrounds were black to match the DAF uniform while the bars and chevrons appeared in either silver-white or gold-yellow. Armbands, worn on the upper right arm, comprised the standard red, white and black swastika design, although they could also include details of the wearer's status and the DAF organisational symbol picked out in white between two similarly coloured bands above the central swastika device.

ABOVE: The men of the DAF were uniformed and had a rank structure. Their ranks were shown by the use of arm chevrons, some with the addition of a distinctive curl on the lower chevron. However, this organisation was not free of periodic changes of rank terms. The chevrons shown here were worn by a DAF-Truppführer (first pattern insignia); a DAF-Gauwerkscharführer as second pattern insignia introduced in 1937; and finally, as a DAF-Arbeitsgruppenführer working in a factory, circa 1938.

RIGHT: Non-German workers employed on war work within the borders of the German Reich would normally wear an identifying badge to show their country of origin. Shown here is a young woman from Denmark operating a machine. She wears what appears to be an armband using the national flag of Denmark.

Youth Organisations

Hitler believed that the Third Reich could only survive for the planned 1,000 years if its young people were indoctrinated in Nazi ideology, and both mentally and physically prepared for struggle. He wanted young Germans to be as 'swift as the greyhound, tough as leather, and hard as Krupp steel' and to this end founded youth movements for both girls and boys. The **Hitlerjugend** (HJ/Hitler Youth), a branch of the Nazi Party, was created for boys but acted as the umbrella organisation for both sexes. The movement underwent a phenomenal rate of growth from just 100,000 members in late 1932 to around 3.5 million by 1935. On the eve of World War II almost every young German male between the ages of 10 and 18 was in the ranks of the Hitler Youth. Baldur von Shirach, the movement's leader from 1933 to 1940, justifiably claimed that 90 percent of all those eligible were members by 1937. Although individuals joined out of real enthusiasm, because of the indoctrination of Nazi ideology at school, parental or even peer-group pressure, the chief reasons for this rapid growth were state compulsion and the suppression of pre-existing rival organisations. In the 18 months after Hitler's accession to power in 1933, numerous rival bodies, such as the Youth League, the Boy Scouts, and various Protestant groups, were effectively disbanded as part of Hitler's Gleichschaltung (co-ordination or unification of the political will) programme to create a Nazi state by sweeping away the existing political and social structures, although many of their leaders took on similar roles in the Hitler Youth. Membership of von Shirach's body was voluntary until December 1936, when the new regulations of the Hitler Youth Law made it compulsory.

Between the ages of 10 and 13 each member of the Hitler Youth was attached to its **Deutsches Jungvolk** (DJ/German Youth) section and was known as a Pimpf.

BELOW LEFT: **From 1 January 1933 when they were first introduced, district arm triangles (Obergauarmdreieck) were, a feature of the uniforms worn by members of the Hitlerjugend (HJ), the Bund Deutscher Mädel (BDM) and the Deutsches Jungvolk (DJ) although their use by the latter was later rescinded. The majority of the black cloth triangles had two lines of Gothic lettering, although there were others produced with a single name such as Landjahr, Akademie, etc and others with a triple row of lettering, Reichs-Deutsche-Jungen Ausland being just one such example. Members of the Hitler Youth had yellow lettering and narrow borders to their arm triangles. The BDM had white lettering and narrow borders. The three examples shown here were for members of the BDM. The upper title 'West' and 'Süd' refers to the BDM Gauverband of the wearer and the lower word the wearer's Obergau, in this case Westmark, Köln-Aachen and Baden. The Baden badge has the tradition bar – in silver Litzen for BDM members – sewn to the lower edge of the triangle. This distinction was introduced to distinguish those units, HJ and BDM, that had been in existence before 1 January 1933. The distinction was extended to those units operating in the Saar prior to 13 January 1935 and later still to those that had been formed in the Sudetenland before 8 February 1938. In the case of the Hitler Youth units their tradition bar strip was yellow.**

BELOW: **As the war progressed and the bombing campaign by the USAAF by day and the RAF by night increased, Allied aircrew were increasingly shot down. Older Hitler Youth members were organised into armed patrols to assist the German police and units of the Army to search out and detain these airmen. These armed HJ units wore a distinguishing cuff-title displaying the gold-yellow lettering HJ-Streifendienst on a black band. Just such a title is shown here being worn on the left forearm of the youth nearest the camera.**

To enter the Jungvolk, the individual undertook a variety of tests. These were chiefly physical – a 60 m dash to be completed in 12 seconds, a 2.75 m long jump, shot putting, and a 72-hour cross-country trek – ideological and pseudo-military. In the ideological sphere, the new recruit was expected to demonstrate a basic understanding of the Nazi creed and sing every verse of the Horst Wessel song, while in the last section he was asked to demonstrate some knowledge of map reading and take part in wargames. On completing these various test the initiate was given a dagger and accepted into the Jungvolk, where training over the next four years focussed on learning various military skills, including semaphore, the laying of telephone wires and arms drill. From 14 to 18 the Jungvolk veterans continued in the Hitler Youth proper, which provided them with a host of activities to develop both mind and body, such as music and hiking trips. These activities were considered a public duty and failure to attend was considered a disgrace. The routine was devised so that HJ members had little time to socialise with their families and thus became prepared for the rigours of military life.

The female equivalent of the Hitler Youth was the **Bund Deutscher Mädel** (BDM/German Girls' League), which had two million members in 1936. Girls aged from 14 were part of the **Jungmädel** (Young Girls) movement and, like their male counterparts, were expected to demonstrate knowledge of Nazi beliefs, show some sporting prowess, and learn supposedly appropriate feminine skills, such as bed making and other household chores. Between 17 and 21 young women attended the activities of the **Glaube und Schönheit** (Faith and Beauty) organisation, which emphasised their physical and cultural well-being but also provided instruction in home-making skills, fashion and beauty. Members were expected to undertake a duty year, usually with urban recruits spending 12 months on a farm while those from the countryside undertook domestic service.

The various youth movements had a full panoply of insignia, the most ubiquitous being their organisational symbol – a lozenge with a central black swastika. It appeared in several forms and was most commonly seen as an armband. There were numerous variously coloured shoulder straps, worn in pairs for the HJ and singly on the right shoulder for the DJ. For the HJ these initially indicated not only the wearer's rank but also his district membership by way of

BDM·OSTEINSATZ

Landdienſt der HJ

coloured edging and additional badges. The system was simplified in 1938 with all straps being black or dark blue, the latter for Marine-HJ. Coloured piping, numbers or letters indicated district membership, while pips or oak leaves in silver-white or gold-yellow were used for rank. The most common DJ shoulder strap was simply black with fine white piping and the wearer's unit and rank, although rank was most commonly indicated by a circular patch with various combinations of chevrons and pips worn on the upper right arm. Rank in the BDM was displayed by badges worn on the left breast consisting of a variation of the Nazi eagle and swastika emblem in silver-white or gold-yellow with various adornments such as edging and oak leaves.

Membership of a particular unit was also indicated by a triangular badge worn on the upper arm consisting of a usually black background with silver-white (BDM) or gold-yellow (HJ and sometimes the DJ) edging with similar coloured Gothic script. The DJ also wore an oval badge on the upper left arm to indicate district membership. All comprised a single lightning bolt rune in either black or white on one of six coloured backgrounds, each of which represented a particular district.

Members were also expected to undertake courses to gain knowledge of certain trades, become proficient in certain skills, and gain some technical skills. Success was indicated by a variety of badges worn on both the left and right arms depending on their particular nature and these came in a variety of shapes, colours and designs. Cuff-titles were worn for several purposes, often related to additional 'voluntary' service or training. For example, those undertaking the year's work in the countryside wore a black title with the wording 'Landdienst der HJ' (Hitler Youth Land Service) in silver-white, while those undertaking the semi-military patrol service wore an armband with the lettering 'HJ-Streifendienst'.

ABOVE: **Hitler Youth shoulder straps underwent a number of changes and modifications between 1933 and 1938. Shown here is a small selection of the 1938 period straps. Colour was utilised on these shoulder straps – in this case bright red being used by the General-HJ. Both the Bann numbers and the edging to the straps, worn in pairs, are in the HJ branch colour. The reverses, underside of the two straps on the right, are shown to view the RZM paper label and also the simple tongue to the strap.**

OPPOSITE, BELOW: **The BDM-Osteinsatz cuff-title (literally BDM Eastern Action) as worn by girls and young women who had volunteered to work in that area during wartime. Worn on the left forearm it was something of a departure from the normal type of HJ-BDM cuff-titles in that it had white lettering and edging on a mid-brown cuff-title.**

The white on black Landdienst der HJ cuff-title was a distinction worn by those members of the Hitler Youth and the BDM who assisted with work on the land.

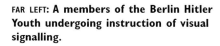

FAR LEFT: **A members of the Berlin Hitler Youth undergoing instruction of visual signalling.**

LEFT: **The HJ emblem.**

BELOW LEFT: **Three very different items worn by members of the Hitlerjugend. The silver-grey wheel on a pink disc was a qualification badge – the Kraftfahrerabzeichen – was worn by those youths who were qualified as Class A to drive a motorised vehicle, something that included a knowledge of driving, vehicle repair, driving laws and road signs, as well as proficiency in driving. This badge was worn on the left forearm.**

The HJ Fire Defence Badge. This sleeve diamond had the German police eagle superimposed on the HJ emblem replacing the swastika. With the addition of red flames it was a wartime distinction worn by those youths who formed part of the HJ Fire Defence units. If the diamond had a narrow carmine-red border it was worn by formation members, narrow white border indicated a leader.

The Wolf's angle rune on an oval of red cloth, sometimes on a red diamond worn horizontally on the left forearm, was worn by those chosen for their ability to act as adjutant to a political leader.

OPPOSITE, ABOVE: **The standard issue Hitler Youth armband, normally worn on the left upper arm.**

OPPOSITE BELOW: **On a main line Berlin railway station, members of the BDM greet soldiers returning from the fronts who are about to proceed on leave. Unlike the Hitler Youth the members of the BDM did not wear an armband. Instead they displayed the HJ diamond on their left upper arm. This same emblem was also used as a sport vest badge.**

133

TOP: The cloth, machine-woven, version of the silver Proficiency Badge for the Hitler Youth (Leistungsabzeichen der Hitlerjugend). This cloth item was worn as a diamond.

TOP RIGHT: The regulation pattern Flak helper's breast badge as worn by Hitler Youth manning AA gun emplacements. The full title of Luftwaffenhelfer-Hitlerjugend was shortened to Luftwaffenhelfer and further to Flakhelfer. It was worn on the right breast of the special blue-grey uniform.

ABOVE: A further selection of the 1938 pattern Hitler Youth shoulder straps. White was the colour appointed to be used by the Patrol Service (Streifendienst), yellow by Signals HJ and the pale blue strap with silver life rune was worn by HJ medical personnel.

BELOW: Three of the four cuff strips, each 20 mm high, worn by both HJ and DJ youths who acted as an attendant for one of four sporting activities.

The green on black H.J.-Schiesswart cuff strip was worn by HJ marksmanship wardens.

The red on black H.J.-Sportwart cuff strip was worn by HJ sports attendants.

The yellow on black Geländesportwart cuff strip was used by HJ field exercise wardens.

The white on black H.J.-Schiwart cuff strip (not illustrated) was worn by HJ ski attendants.

These cuff strips were introduced in November 1936 and were worn on the lower left forearm just above the seam of the shirt cuff. It was possible to wear more than one strip and when this happened there was a gap of 20 mm between each strip.

BOTTOM: Two pairs and a single shoulder strap of the 1938 pattern as worn by Hitler Youths who were in motorised units.

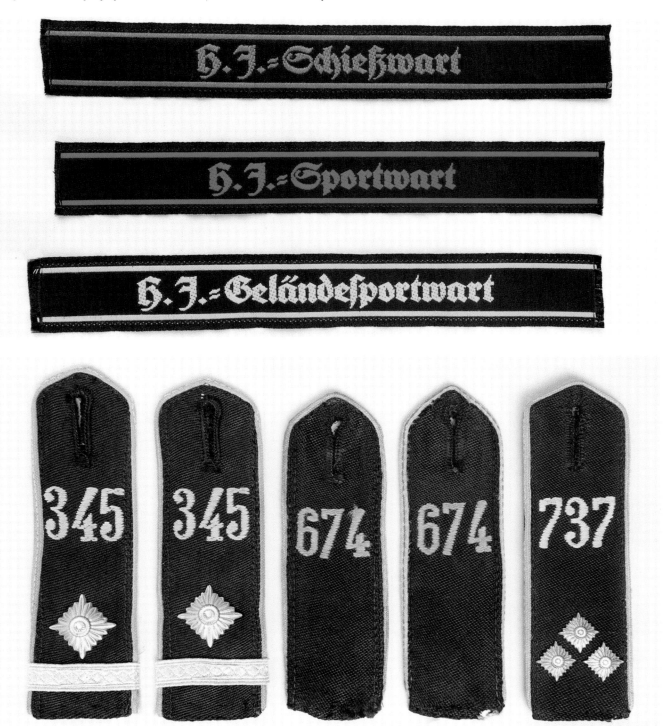

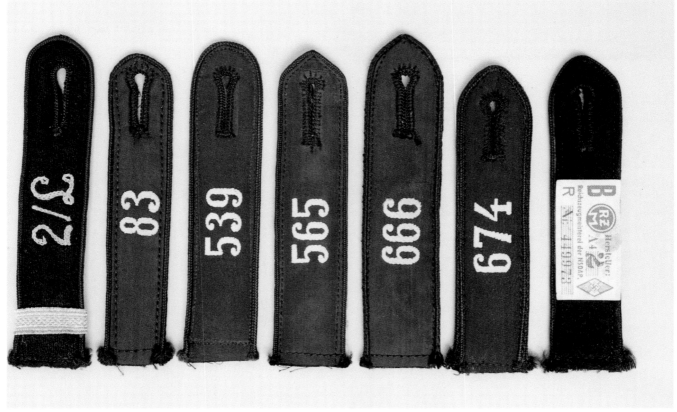

LEFT: **The arm badge for a senior Hitler Youth medical orderly. This badge was introduced in January 1941, and was usually worn on the left forearm.**

BELOW: **The machine-woven cloth version of the DJ Proficiency Badge (DJ-Leistungsabzeichen).**

BOTTOM: **Under the guidance of an adult HJ instructor, members of the Signals-Hitler Youth (Nachrichten-HJ) are trained on teleprinter ticker-tape machines.**

OPPOSITE, ABOVE: **A selection of four early-1933 pattern Hitler Youth shoulder straps. The distinctive feature of these early straps was their tan-coloured material, officially referred to as khaki brown, together with the use of coloured letters or numbers stitched into the straps. From left to right: the first was for a youth from Oberbann 4, light blue being the colour appointed for this Oberbann. The letter 'L' is believed to stand for 'instructor'.**

The second was worn by a youth Bann number 123 in Oberbann 1, red being their Oberbann colour.

The third was for a HJ member from Unterbann V, in Bann 285 from the Oberbann 3, green being their colour.

The fourth, devoid of insignia, is something of a mystery. It was probably worn by a youth from Oberbann 3.

OPPOSITE, BELOW: **A selection of seven shoulder straps for wear by members of the DJ. The numerals, and in one instance a letter, are stitched into the strap along its length, contrary to the normal practice of displaying the insignia across the width of the strap. As these straps were only worn singly on the right shoulder, this method of display meant that, when viewed from the front, the numerals read from left to right. Straps were first introduced into the DJ in April 1935 and there were eventually two patterns. From left to right: the first is a first-pattern strap. The white chain-stitched insignia 2/L is believed to stand for a youth serving in 2nd Stamm from Bann 'Jungsturm' based on Munich. The following six straps were of the second-pattern introduction, all piped in black cord and all bearing their Jungbann number in white. The final strap shows the underside of a strap affixed with the obligatory RZM paper label.**

ABOVE: **Portrait of Dr Jutta Rüdiger, head of the German Girls' League (Reichreferentin BDM).**

LEFT: **A propaganda portrait of an Untergauführerin in the BDM working at her desk.**

ABOVE RIGHT: **Pupils undergoing instruction at the Waffen-SS School of Music based at Brunswick (Braunschweig).**

RIGHT: **Members of the Hitler Youth and the Deutsches Jungvolk displaying intense concentration while being instructed in the use of a machine gun by an Army officer.**

ABOVE: Six of the DJ Sigrune arm badges introduced in 1933. These coloured badges were worn by the DJ equivalents of NCOs and officers – from Stabsmitglieder to Stammführer – serving a similar purpose to rank insignia. They were worn on the upper left sleeve of the tan summer shirt and the dark blue winter jacket, the badge being positioned 5 cm above the wearer's elbow. The colour of the disc and that of the Sigrune was associated with the wearer's Oberbann. From left to right: top row – white on red Oberbann 1; black on yellow Oberbann 2; white on green Oberbann 3; next row – white on blue Oberbann 4; white on black Oberbann 5; and black on white Oberbann 6.

RIGHT: The type of armband worn by members of the Deutsches Jungvolk. Similar to the armband worn by members of the Hitlerjugend, on this armband a black rune replaced the swastika emblem.

OPPOSITE: Side drummers from a National Political Education School at a parade held at Naumburg. All wear the single, DJ pattern shoulder strap displaying the initial letters NPEA and all wear musicians' wings. Two of these young boys are wearing the metal version of the DJ Proficiency badge.

Home Defence

When Hitler came to power in 1933, he immediately set about preparing Germany's armed forces and its civilians for war. One of the key efforts on the home front was to provide a measure of security and assistance to ordinary people in the case of air attacks by any enemy. As the war progressed the importance of the various organisations grew markedly in significance. Aside from elements of the Luftwaffe and the paramilitary fire police, the Nazis deployed four uniformed bodies to protect ordinary German citizens and their property from the unrelenting Allied strategic bombing offensive. These were the **Reichsluftschutzbund** (RLB/National Air Defence League) formed in late April 1933, the **Sicherheits und Hilfsdienst** (SHD/Security and Assistance Service), the **Wasserstrassenluftschutz** (Waterways Air Protection Service), and the **Luftschutz Warndienst** (LSW/Air Raid Warning Service). All wore grey-blue uniforms, but differed markedly in their insignia

The RLB's organisational emblem, which was worn on the left forearm, consisted of a naturalistic silver-white eagle in flight holding a similarly coloured stylised starburst on which was superimposed a swastika; the background material was grey-blue cloth to match the uniform colour and was sometimes worn with chevrons in silver-white which might indicate rank or, more probably, length of service. Members of the RLB had a single shoulder strap on the right and two matching collar patches of lilac material. For ordinary ranks the patches were plain but carried various adornments – triangular pips, L-shaped bars, cording edges and wreaths of various designs – in either silver-white or gold-yellow for the various grades of seniority. A similar pattern was followed for the shoulder straps. For junior ranks they were lilac edged black while seniority was denoted by increasingly complex cording in silver-white, gold-yellow or a combination of the two. Unlike his officers and men the head of the RLB wore white shoulder patches and shoulder straps with gold-yellow adornment. Various patterns of armbands were worn on the upper left arm. The first comprised grey-blue material with a central starburst motif over which lay the Gothic letters RLB above a similarly coloured swastika. Silver-white edging at top and bottom of the armband may have indicated rank. A second pattern was simpler – a plain light blue background with a starburst in silver-white under a black swastika.

The SHD and LSW wore matching pairs of shoulder straps and collar patches and these were identified by dark green material. Shoulder straps were simply edged in a lighter green for lower ranks but became increasingly complex with seniority. Adornments denoting rank included white and green edging, and pips and twisted cording in silver-white and gold-yellow. Collar patches contained indications of both the formation and general rank. In the former case this consisted of abbreviations of the two names SHD and LSW in white or silver-white Gothic script, in the latter case seniority was indicated by white and green edging for ordinary ranks and silver-white for higher grades.

Both formations created a range of identifying armbands worn on the upper left arm and many were extremely basic, identifying in the briefest way either membership of the body or a specific role within it. One for the LSW, for example, comprised a green background with a bold letter L in black, while another, possibly worn by observers, carried a bold letter W in white on a red background. LSW personnel were also sometimes identified by a cuff-title worn on the left forearm, which consisted of a dark green band with the Gothic lettering 'L.S. Warndienst' in silver-white. From 1941 the SHD introduced a series of specialist badges that were mostly worn on the upper left arm, although they were sometimes carried on the forearm. The SHD had five distinct branches – fire-fighting, repair and maintenance, veterinary, decontamination and medical – and members of each wore identifying arm badges. All consisted of an oval design and, with the exception of that of the medical service, which comprised a snake twisted around a staff, carried a Gothic letter to provide an abbreviated reference to the sub-division. The arm badge denoting personnel of the Entgiftungsdienst für im Gasspüren und Entgiften Ausgebildete decontamination branch carried a necessarily simple Gothic G. The oval badges and letters themselves came in various colour combinations, although all were edged in green. The decontamination section's emblem consisted of a yellow background with the Gothic G in black.

The Wasserstrassenluftschutz was founded in 1942 and performed functions similar to the LSW but with responsibilities for Germany's rivers, waterways and harbours. Rank was identified by matching pairs of both shoulder straps and collar patches, although the process was somewhat simplified by having separate shoulder straps for the organisation's 12 specified ranks but only four sets of collar patches. Collar patches had a light blue background and all carried a rope and anchor motif in silver-white or gold-yellow, while rank was indicated by differently styled and coloured edgings and the addition of various numbers of stylised waves in either silver-white or gold-yellow to the anchor. Shoulder straps consisted of plain blue material or various designs in white and blue, with the addition of various bars and sunbursts to indicate seniority.

BELOW: As the war went on, the Sicherheits und Hilfsdienst, the Security and Assistance Service, increasingly found its main task to assist the civilian population in the event of air raids.

During 1941 SHD units specialist badges were introduced. These were worn on the left upper arm of the uniform, and occasionally on the left forearm. Three are featured:

The white letter 'F' on a red oval within a green oval frame indicated a member of the SHD Fire Fighting Service (Feuerlöschdienst).

The white serpent entwined around a white staff set on a pale blue-green edged oval was worn by SHD Medical personnel (Sanitätsdienst).

The black Gothic letter 'G' on a yellow oval within a green border was worn by the men of SHD decontamination squads (Entgiftungsdienst für im Gasspüren und Entgiften Ausgebildete).

OPPOSITE: A pair of collar patches (TOP) as worn by officers of the Luftschutz und Warndienst (Air Protection and Warning Service) and (BELOW) for officers of the Sicherheits und Hilfsdienst.

ABOVE: A member of the Bonn Luftschutz Warndienst keeps a watch for the approach of enemy aircraft. He wears the dark green LWD collar patches and the Luftschutz emblem as an arm badge on his left upper arm.

OPPOSITE, ABOVE: The first pattern RLB armband of the type worn by members of the National Air Defence League. The emblem used on these armbands and also on the flags used by the league was changed before the war to one that had just the starburst with a large central swastika, the letters 'RLB' being dropped.

OPPOSITE, BELOW: A 'set' of rank insignia as worn by the Chief of Staff of the RLB, holding the rank of General-Haupt-Luftschutz-Führer. The two shoulder straps are different. The lower end of the strap on the left was sewn into the shoulder seam of the wearer's tunic or coat whereas the other strap had stiffened 'prongs' which allowed the strap to be attached to shoulder loops on a heavy-duty coat, such as an officer's leather coat.

LEFT: From the top – a shoulder strap and collar patch for an RLB Luftschutz-Führer; next, a pair of collar patches and a single shoulder strap (of a pair) for the RLB senior officer rank of Stabsluftschutz-Führer.

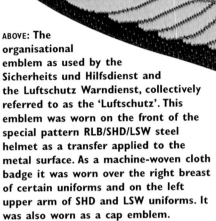

ABOVE: The organisational emblem as used by the Sicherheits und Hilfsdienst and the Luftschutz Warndienst, collectively referred to as the 'Luftschutz'. This emblem was worn on the front of the special pattern RLB/SHD/LSW steel helmet as a transfer applied to the metal surface. As a machine-woven cloth badge it was worn over the right breast of certain uniforms and on the left upper arm of SHD and LSW uniforms. It was also worn as a cap emblem.

RIGHT: The second pattern armband for wear by ordinary members.

BELOW RIGHT: A demonstration given by a member of the Reichsluftschutzbund, the German Air Raid Protection Service, on the dangers of phosphorous bombs. The colour of this organisation's collar patches and the underlay and/or piping to their shoulder straps was lilac. The emblem for the RLB can be seen displayed on the left forearm of the junior officer here shown about to demonstrate the deadly effect of phosphorous bombs.

LEFT: A dark blue armband with the letter 'O' formed from a length of white tape. This band was worn by members of the Luftschutz but its purpose is unknown.

BELOW LEFT: A dark blue armband with a large form of a rank star in white. The purpose of this particular armband is unknown but may well represent a form of rank insignia.

BELOW: A red armband with the white capital letter 'W' or 'M' depending on which way up the band was worn. If it was worn to show the letter 'W' it could have been worn by a guard or watchman, W = Wächter. If the letter is 'M' it could have stood for despatch rider, M = Meldefahrer, or a runner or messenger, M = Meldegänger.

Organisation Todt

The **Organisation Todt** (OT) was created as a semi-military body to oversee aspects of the Nazi Party's rearmament programme and its preparations for war. It was chiefly responsible for the construction of various types of military installations and a network of modern highways, the Reichsautobahnen, that were suitable for the use of heavy military traffic, particularly tanks and other armoured vehicles. From 1936, the OT was also engaged in implementing Hitler's Four-Year Plan, which focussed on expanding Nazi Germany's economic base, including certain key industries such as chemicals, engineering and mining. The organisation's first head was Dr Fritz Todt, a World War I veteran who had trained as a construction engineer and joined the Nazi Party in 1923. His appointment was announced in 1933. Todt was killed in an air crash during a visit to Hitler's headquarters at Rastenburg in East Prussia on 8 February 1942, and Albert Speer took over his responsibilities.

Before World War II OT workers were engaged on building the motorway network, which was planned to consist of some 7,200 miles (9,920 km) of highway and had been initiated by the Weimar Republic. The first section was opened between Bonn and Cologne in 1932, a year before Hitler assumed power, and he ordered Todt to oversee a vast expansion in the programme in September 1933. An initial 30,000 men were engaged in the work and the figure rose to more than 70,000 over the following years. Most of the four-lane highways actually built, some 1,800 miles (2,880 km) by 1938, ran from west to east so that the Nazi leadership could fight a war on two fronts if it became necessary by transferring troops rapidly between the two potential war zones. The OT's other major pre-war projects were the fortifications of the Westwall, which ran from Luxembourg to

ABOVE: **Luftwaffe Generalmajor Adolf Galland (left) in conversation with Albert Speer, September 1943.**

Amongst Speer's many appointments was his position of Reichsminister for Armaments and War Production. He was also Chief of the Organisation Todt, a post to which he was appointed on the death of the previous chief, Dr Fritz Todt. Speer is seen here wearing a simplified brown uniform to which has been added twisted silver cording around the edge of the collar. The OT swastika armband was of the type worn by senior officers of this organisation.

Switzerland and protected Germany's border with France. The work began in 1938 and some one million men – many simply ordered to take part – were employed at one time or another in a task that continued at various rates until the area was overrun by the Allies during the winter of 1944–45.

From 1938 to shortly before the invasion of Poland in September 1939, the bulk of OT workers were provided by non-military contractors and wore normal civilian clothing, while leadership and direction on OT projects came from uniformed members of the military or the Reichsarbeitsdienst (RAD/State Labour Service). After this date attempts were made to 'militarise' the OT with workers and managers being identified by badge designs indicating the organisation, rank, service and speciality variously worn on the collar, shoulders and arms. A range of organisational bands worn on the upper left arm was first introduced from 1940 and, for a time, they were the main means of identifying OT membership. These varied in complexity: the designs for the non-uniformed personnel varied in background colour with 'O.T.' in black with possibly a unit number beneath, while uniformed members were identified by more complex designs, usually including a grey background, a black Nazi eagle and 'Org. Todt' in Gothic script, and one or more narrow red bands. Other embellishments were also added to the armband as were means of showing the wearer's membership of either the OT's Bau (construction service) or Transport branch, with the latter being identified by two hollow black triangles. A new range of rank insignia was introduced in 1942 and gave greater prominence to chevrons, shoulder straps and collar patches. This system was modified for the final time in 1943, when the shoulder straps were dispensed with and replaced by new forms of chevrons, patches and armbands.

From April 1942 the appropriate personnel also wore oval badges that denoted their particular specialisation if on their right forearm or service branch on their left. In the former case these consisted of an appropriate symbol in white usually on a black or brown background. In the case of service branches, these followed a similar pattern of symbols in white but usually on a khaki-green background.

The **Technische Nothilfe** (TeNo/Technical Emergency Corps) was a paramilitary organisation with responsibility for specialist construction work. Its organisational symbol was worn on the upper left arm and comprised an eagle and swastika design with a letter N and hammer within a cog wheel superimposed over it. Membership of the body was also indicated by an armband worn on the left arm consisting of a black band with 'Technische Nothilfe' in Gothic lettering picked out in either silver-white or grey, while other lettering indicated the recruit's date of recruitment surrounded by oak leaves in gold-yellow. TeNo rank insignia underwent several changes between 1937 and 1945 but followed the usual pattern of shoulder straps and collar patches to indicate branch of service (red for the civil air defence division, for example) as well as rank and unit. Arm badges consisted of a black circle on which appeared the organisational cogwheel within which appeared Gothic lettering or a symbol to indicate the wearer's trade. A further badge, consisting of an arrow-like device in black and white on the upper left arm, indicated staff or graduates of TeNo's training school.

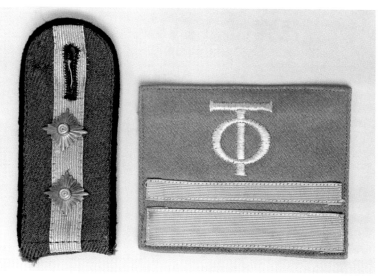

ABOVE: **A single shoulder strap and arm rank patch for personnel of the OT. The strap was worn by an OT-Haupttruppführer of the Construction and Accommodation Control branch, black being their branch colour displayed as piping to the strap. This was the commonest of all the OT branch colours, the others being dark blue for medical branch, white for the Equipment, Provisions and Messing section, brown for the Propaganda wing, lemon yellow for Signals Sections, green for Administration and carmine for Musicians and Musical Detachments. The arm patch worn on the upper right arm of the work uniform displayed the wearer's OT rank (not established).**

OPPOSITE, BELOW: **The basic swastika armband worn together with a narrow grey band bearing the black letters ORG. TODT. Worn together, and frequently stitched together, this was the official emblem used by workers of the Organisation Todt.**

RIGHT AND BELOW RIGHT: Two **OT** armbands, 1940 period, worn by non-uniformed OT workers. The small black printed number is thought to represent the OT unit number.

BELOW: Somewhat elderly Technical and Emergency Service recruits undergoing instruction on a theodolite. All the men under instruction wear the grey coloured fatigue uniforms without any visible rank insignia and only the standard issue TeNo arm eagle. The instructor wears the dark blue-black greatcoat complete with collar patches, shoulder straps, TeNo arm eagle plus the special TeNo arrowhead badge. This last item was worn by those persons who have successfully passed through the TeNo School of Instruction.

FAR LEFT: **A pair and two single collar patches of the pattern introduced in 1943 and worn by Staff Leaders of the Organisation Todt. The pair of patches (TOP) were worn by those construction leaders holding the rank of OT-Bauleiter, OT-Stabsfrontführer or OT-Oberstabsarzt. Below are two single patches. On the right one of a pair as worn by an OT-Oberbauleiter, OT-Oberstabsfrontführer or OT-Oberfeldarzt. On the left the other single strap, one of a pair, was worn by OT staff leaders with the ranks of OT-Hauptbauleiter, OT-Oberstabsfrontführer and OT-Oberstarzt.**

LEFT: **Officers' collar patches of 1943–45. The top two are a pair worn by an OT-Oberbauführer; the bottom one that worn by an OT-Hauptbauführer. The device was called a Wehrbau.**

BELOW LEFT: **The left-hand plain collar patches were worn with chevrons to indicate OT ranks from OT-Vorarbeiter to OT-Hauptsanitäter. When worn with a single red rank chevron worn on the upper right arm this indicated the rank of OT-Vorarbeiter and OT-Stammsanitäter. Two red arm chevrons were used by the ranks of OT-Meister and OT-Obersanitäter. The two final ranks in the OT under leader group of ranks were OT-Obermeister and OT-Hauptsanitäter. They wore the plain collar patches but each with three red arm chevrons. The OT collar patch with a single white metal pip was worn by OT-Truppführer and OT-Sanitäts-Truppführer. The patches bearing three metal pips set in a triangular form were worn by an OT-Haupttruppführer and an OT-Sanitäts-Haupttruppführer.**

BOTTOM LEFT: **Speciality and Service insignia worn on the right forearm as small circular cloth patches displaying a particular symbol were introduced in April 1942. They were a visible recognition of the skills and qualifications of the work personnel and OT leaders. Left to right from top row: carpenter (Zimmermann), bricklayer-mason (Maurer), next believed to be for a mechanic, OT driver (Kraftfahrer), and finally an unestablished badge, probably for a surveyor. There were other similar patches for other skills and qualifications but they are not shown here.**

LEFT: Two pairs of shoulder straps and a single arm eagle as worn by members of the TeNo. The upper pair of straps were in use from 1937 to 1945 and during that period the TeNo rank terms were altered three times. For the 1937-40 period these straps were worn by a TN-Anwarter and TN-Nothelfer, For the 1941-42 ranks these were worn by the rank of TN-Nothelfer only, and in the 1942-43 the straps were being worn by a TN-Anwarter and a TN-Mann. The two lower straps, which form a pair, were worn by a TN-Obervormann throughout the three periods of rank term changes. The triangular badge was the TeNo arm eagle, worn on the upper left arm of dark blue-black uniform tunic and greatcoat. The swastika was superimposed with the TeNo symbol consisting of the conjoined letters TN set inside a cog-wheel, a symbol clearly seen on the armband in the next illustration.

LEFT: A special arm badge introduced in January 1942 for wear by members of German Army technical units who had formerly been members of the TeNo. It was worn on the upper right arm of the Army field and service uniform and on the greatcoat. The badge is only known to have been produced as a BeVo quality badge.

OPPOSITE, BELOW: The issue armband for wear by TeNo personnel.

BELOW: Cuff-titles, from top to bottom – first a tradition title worn by those serving in the TeNo in the 1920s; next, two examples of the ordinary cuff-title worn by TeNo members in the Nazi period.

Police

ABOVE: The ubiquitous German police arm eagle badge. This design of badge, introduced in July 1936 when the new police uniforms were brought into wear, was produced in a number of different qualities with background colours to match the wearer's uniform cloth, and embroidered in colours that corresponded with the wearer's branch colour combinations. With the addition of the names of towns, cities and localities the number of these arm badges was even more prolific. The police eagle badge was worn on the upper left sleeve.

Shown here is a standard badge for wear by a police officer below the rank of general. The quality is of the type manufactured as a woven badge but in silver-aluminium threads.

As with many other administrative and official branches of the German state, the Nazis undertook a thorough root-and-branch reorganisation of the country's numerous semi-independent and often specialist police forces, each of which had a clearly defined function or area of responsibility, after they had achieved power in January 1933. The aim was to bring them under direct control at national level and tie them closer to the new state. The policy was part of the process of Gleichschaltung (unification or co-ordination of the political will) that was designed to sweep away or transform the structures of the former Weimar Republic and replace them with new or revised bodies that were organised and run along lines acceptable to the Nazi leadership. Although the various police forces continued to undertake their traditional duties, Hitler also expanded the state's law enforcement agencies by initially directing elements of the SA, Stahlhelm and SS to perform auxiliary police duties immediately after assuming the chancellorship and in 1934 he went further by creating the **Sicherheitsdienst** (SD – Security Service) under Reinhard Heydrich, which was entrusted with the security of the Third Reich and, in the form of the **Geheime Staatspolizei** (Gestapo – Secret State Police), had extensive powers that went far beyond the pre-existing forces. These old police forces continued to preserve law and order in the generally accepted sense but also supported the work of the Nazi Party's own state security forces to which they were effectively subordinated. The Nazis also took over and expanded the pre-existing **Landespolizeigruppen** and these police units, which already had a paramilitary role, took on a role that was increasingly military in nature rather than purely one of law enforcement.

Several distinct police bodies were affected by the new legislation introduced by the Nazis – among these were the **Bahnschutzpolizei** (Railway Protection Police); the **Feuerschutzpolizei** (Fire Protection Police); the **Gendarmerie** based in rural areas; the **Grenzpolizei** (Border Police); the **Marine-Küstenpolizei** (Naval Coastal Police); the **Motorisierten Gendarmerie Bereitschaft** (Motorised Gendarmerie Emergency Service) that patrolled the motorway system; the **Polizei Medizinal Beamte** (Police Medical Service), the **Polizei Verwaltungs Beamte** (Police Administration Service); the **Polizei-Veterinärbeamte** (Police Veterinary Service); the **Schutzpolizei des Gemeinden** (District or Community Protection Police); the **Schutzpolizei des Reiches** (Reich Protection Police); and the **Wasserschutzpolizei** (Waterways Protection Police). The key legislation was introduced in January 1934, when the powers previously exercised by the country's various Länder (states) to control and direct police activities were surrendered to the national government, thereby centralising and extending the Nazi Party's control and direction of the country's law enforcement agencies. As part of this ongoing process the Nazi hierarchy decreed that certain aspects of the forces' existing uniforms and insignia should be modified to reflect their new status within the Third Reich.

154

By 1936 the process of transformation was well underway and this was reflected in the partial militarisation of police ranks – they mirrored in many respects those of the Army and the Waffen-SS – and the introduction of new branch of service colours known as Truppenfarben for shoulder straps and collar patches, which were generally worn in matching pairs by most of the previously mentioned bodies. For example, members of the Community Police were identified by wine red until it merged with the Reich Protection Police and took on its Truppenfarbe; Fire Protection Police were identified by carmine; the Motorised Gendarmerie Emergency Service wore white; the Police Administration Service wore light grey; the Police Medical Service light blue; the Police Veterinary Service wore black; the Reich Protection Police wore light green; the Gendermarie wore orange; and the Waterways Protection Police, which did not make use of collar patches, wore bright yellow. Shoulder straps edged in these colours also provided details of the wearer's rank, length of service and in some cases trade, through various combinations of pips in either silver-white or gold-yellow, various combinations and styles of cording, and letters, the last frequently used to denote a specialist role, such as a capital A to indicate an Oberstabsapotheker.

The 1936 reforms particularly impacted on the Gendarmerie, Schutzpolizei des Gemeinden, Schutzpolizei des Reiches and the Wasserschutzpolizei, as well as the auxiliary **Gendarmerie-Bereitschaften** (Rural Standby Police). Revised uniforms and insignia were introduced for all of these bodies and the new patterns were applied to all ranks. A revised organisational emblem was introduced for most of the various police forces which comprised a new eagle badge that was worn on the upper left arm at the midpoint between elbow and shoulder. These new badges were produced in three qualities, each of which was appropriate to either ordinary ranks, junior officers and their superiors. The central design comprised the traditional state eagle with outstretched wings holding the wreathed swastika in both talons, with both the eagle and swastika being encompassed by a larger wreath. The colour of a particular design, at least for lower ranks, corresponded to the particular Truppenfarbe of the formation to which the wearer belonged. Officers generally tended to wear a similar motif but in either silver-white for junior grades and gold-yellow for their highest-ranking personnel, although the Wasserschutzpolizei did not follow this system and all ranks wore a gold-yellow eagle in various qualities of finish. It was also common for lower grades and junior officers to carry details of their service district on the badge above the larger wreath encircling the eagle. Its colour matched that of the eagle motif. The designs mostly appeared on a large oval background cloth appropriate to the colour of the wearer's tunic, most frequently field grey or dark blue/black, although the background was sometimes seen in white to match the tunic temporarily worn when performing traffic-control duties. The exception to the aforementioned organisational/national emblem was that worn by members of the Bahnschutzpolizei. This, in contrast, comprised a notably thinner and more naturalistic eagle again holding the wreathed swastika in its talons, but dispensed with the larger surrounding wreath that was common to the other police formations.

ABOVE: **The arm badge as worn by police personnel up to the rank of Leutnant of the Schutzpolizei, the Protection Police, green being their branch colour.**

ABOVE: **Arm badge as worn by personnel below officer rank of the Schutzpolizei der Gemeinden (Municipal Protection Police).**

BELOW: **Polizeioberwachtmeister Becker with his Great Dane Crino von der Barenau. Oberwachtmeister Becker was a member of the Landespolizeigruppe General Goering, one of the early police formations permitted to Germany under the Treaty of Versailles.**

Cuff-titles worn by the police performed several functions. First, they might simply identify the wearer's membership of a particular sub-division. The Motorised Gendarmerie, for example, wore the title 'Motorisierte Gendarmerie' in Gothic script on their lower left arm above the cuff. This comprised a tan brown band with the lettering in silver-white, and officer grades were marked out from ordinary ranks and non-commissioned officers by the addition of a similarly coloured edging. The system of differentiating between officers and other ranks was most extensive in the Bahnschutzpolizei from 1941 when separate titles were introduced to identify both individual and groups of ranks. From 1941 personnel could wear any one of the six different titles that were used to identify five groups of ranks, which in total were made up of 14 individual ranks. Second, titles might simply name the particular unit to which the wearer belonged and it was again not uncommon for officers and men to be differentiated by the type of thread used and the addition of edgings. Third, cuff-titles were used to indicate that the policeman was on attachment. If they were serving with the armed forces outside the borders of the Third Reich, for example, a title bearing the words 'Deutsche Wehrmacht' was commonly used.

Proficiency badges were comparatively rare items for police personnel and not widely issued, with generally only members of the rural Gendarmerie and the Reich Protection Police being eligible for the awards following their introduction by the Nazis in August 1937. In both cases they were worn on the left forearm of the police tunic and consisted of a mid-green background circular or oval-shaped cloth patch. Various devices in silk or cotton were superimposed onto the background patch in either a lighter green thread for the Schutzpolizei or orange-red for the Gendarmerie in the case of lower ranks, while officers carried the same devices but rendered in silver wire to reflect their status. The emblems themselves were often standard identification symbols found in other state organisations. For example, a steering wheel represented a qualified driver, a horseshoe indicated a trained farrier, while a lightning bolt indicated a communications expert.

One of the more uncommon badges of the Nazi period was awarded to members of specially chosen police units operating within the Third Reich that had been identified as upholding the traditions of formations that had served and maintained order in Germany's former overseas colonies, all of which had been surrendered to the Allies under the provisions of the Treaty of Versailles at the end of World War I. Generally known as a tradition badge, this was a shield-like design that had a white background edged in black onto which was superimposed a narrow black cross. The resulting design was finished by the addition of a representation of the Southern Cross consisting of five white five-pointed stars on a bright red background, which was positioned in the shield's upper left quarter from the viewer's perspective. The award was officially titled the Kreuz des Südens and was attached to the lower left forearm about one centimetre above the cuff.

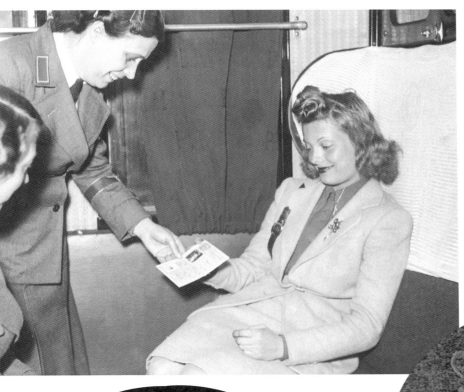

LEFT: **A female member of the German Customs Service checking the identity cards of rail travellers. Customs came within the jurisdiction of the German police.**

BELOW LEFT: **The arm eagle badge worn by all rank grades below officer status of the German Fire Protection Police operating at a factory. Rose pink was the branch colour allotted to the Fire Protection Police.**

BELOW: **The arm badge worn by personnel below officer rank from the City of Munich Schutzpolizei.**

OPPOSITE, ABOVE LEFT: **Badge for a Schutzpolizei der Gemeinden München (Munich).**

OPPOSITE, ABOVE RIGHT: **An arm eagle for a member of the Fire Protection Police based on Brest. It is believed that this particular badge was worn by the Fire Police protecting the U-boat pens at the French port of Brest.**

OPPOSITE, BELOW: **A meeting was held in Berlin on 28 October 1942 between Reichsminister Dr Goebbels and the head of the Italian Carabinieri, seen here being greeted, amongst others, by German police officers upon his arrival at the Berlin Bahnhof.**

LEFT: **Karl Demelhuber, SS-Obergruppenführer und Generalleutnant der Polizei, commander of the Waffen-SS in occupied Holland. He was one of the oldest officers in the Waffen-SS. He is seen here at a wartime winter sports event.**

LEFT: **The Water Protection Police arm eagle. Yellow was their branch colour and, fittingly, their uniforms were of dark navy blue cloth.**

OPPOSITE: **Members of a police sports team taking part in a game of basketball. The police sports vest emblem is clearly seen.**

BELOW LEFT: **The arm eagle badge as worn by a Fire Protection Officer of a factory Fire Protection Police unit.**

BELOW RIGHT: **The arm badge worn by Rural Protection Police based on Klagenfurt. Orange was the colour appointed to be used by the Gendarmerie.**

ABOVE: The arm badge worn by other ranks of the Protection Police for the city of Frankfurt am Main.

ABOVE RIGHT: The police eagle arm badge for wear by the Protection Police of Frankfurt an der Oder in eastern Germany.

RIGHT: Hand-embroidered police arm eagle of blue-grey material believed to be Factory Police.

OPPOSITE: Berlin police officers setting up a mobile siren as part of an air raid defence exercise. The shape of insignia worn on their caps and the collar patches visible on the figure on the right shows that this is a prewar photograph.

OPPOSITE: **A demonstration by a member of the Protection Police on how to tackle a burning phosphorus bomb.**

LEFT AND BELOW LEFT: **Two examples of the Protection Police sports vest emblem, green being the colour for the Schutzpolizei des Reiches.**

BELOW: **Women had been employed within the organisation the German police before the outbreak of war, mainly as office personnel and female warders responsible for women prisoners. However, the necessities of warfare drew even more women into the organisation, many serving in the Fire Protection Police. Shown here is one such woman wearing protective clothing and a Fire Police helmet operating the controls of a water pump.**

ABOVE: **A heavy mortar protected within a purpose-built trench being operated by men of the Waffen-SS Police Division.**

RIGHT: **Arm eagle badge as worn by the members below officer rank of the Gendarmerie, the Rural Police.**

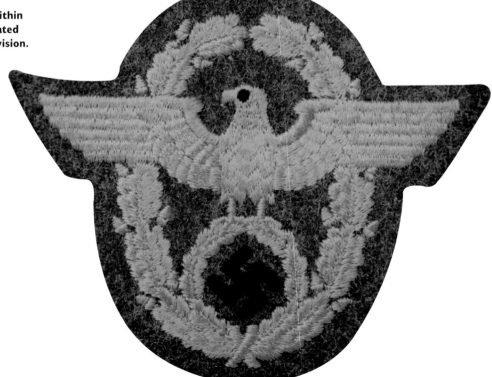

LEFT: **Rural Police stationed in mountainous areas of the Reich had qualified mountaineers amongst their ranks. These persons were entitled to the police version of the Edelweiss arm badge.**

BELOW: **Members of a Postal Protection unit (Postschutz) relax in front of the camera. Their 'arm-of-service colour' was orange and they wore a distinctive arm badge on their left upper arm consisting of an eagle and swastika emblem with lightening bolts emanating from either side.**

ABOVE: **Two examples of the police cap insignia.**

RIGHT: **A female member of the German police and, as indicated by the driving wheel badge on the cuff of her left forearm, a qualified driver. She was photographed soon after being taken into custody as a prisoner of war.**

OPPOSITE: **The official photograph taken of the new police uniforms introduced by the National Socialist authorities in the mid-1930s.**

Volkssturm

ABOVE: **A elderly member of a Volkssturm unit wearing one of a number of semi-official armbands.**

BELOW RIGHT: **The official issue Volkssturm armband.**

By the autumn of 1944 the Allies were rapidly closing on the borders of Nazi Germany from both west and east. German casualties during the year had been enormous, and after more than five years of war suitable replacements were in short supply. To offset this growing numerical inferiority, the Nazi hierarchy ordered the formation of militia units, the Volkssturm, to bolster their home defence, particularly against the Red Army during its drive into the heart of the Third Reich in the spring of 1945 and the subsequent Battle of Berlin. Orders for the creation of the Volkssturm were first issued on 18 October 1944, and the locally raised units officially comprised males aged between 16 and 60, most previously excluded from military service because of their youthfulness, age or lack of the appropriate level of fitness. In practice also both older and younger recruits than the specified limits served in the ranks. Men were frequently sworn in en masse at open air ceremonies before commencing what for most would be a brief military career defending their local area. Rudimentary training was sometimes offered but uniforms were rare with many members wearing civilian dress or their own military-style attire, and only limited equipment was available, chiefly small arms, machine guns, and the single-shot Panzerfaust anti-tank weapon. Officers were provided by other Nazi organisations, including the Hitler Youth, NSKK, SA and SS.

Given the parlous state of the Third Reich's economy and the limited manufacturing resources available, only a basic effort was made to provide the Volkssturm units with appropriate insignia. The growing military crisis hindered any co-ordinated efforts to mass-produce suitable emblems, although it was deemed essential to identify the Volkssturm as members of the official armed forces and the authorities decreed that recruits should be identified by an armband worn on the upper left arm. The official version comprised the national colours of red, black and white displayed in horizontal bands of varying thickness. The wider central band had a black background with the Nazi eagle and the lettering 'Deutscher Volkssturm Wehrmacht' on two lines picked out in white. Although this design was the ideal, many Volkssturm members made do with cruder, often locally produced, designs on the same theme that made use of what was immediately available. These came in a variety of styles, but most were stencilled in black paint or waterproof ink on to whatever suitable material had been provided. The only common feature was the 'Deutscher Volkssturm Wehrmacht' lettering and the eagle.

German Red Cross

Although the Nazis tended to shun most internationally recognised organisations, they did maintain membership of the Red Cross. Under their leadership, the **Deutsches Rotes Kreuz** (DRK/German Red Cross) was transformed into a wholly recognised subsection of the state and recognisable as such by the clothing worn and insignia carried by those serving in its ranks. The organisation was open to both men and women, with the former wearing military attire and the latter generally wearing variations of traditional nursing uniform. The DRK's organisational emblem, a variation of the Nazi state emblem, consisted of a white circle outlined in black and featured a black eagle with a swastika in white on its chest and holding a red cross in its talons. The standard DRK armband, which was worn by all personnel, was carried on the upper left arm and came in a variety of forms. Used to identify both uniformed personnel and volunteers in civilian clothing, the simplest consisted of a red cross on a white background but others incorporated lettering in either Gothic or Roman script, or a mixture of both, positioned above or all around the central cross. The lettering was either just the organisational name or might also include the home district and subsection of the particular unit.

Male members of the Deutsches Rotes Kreuz wore pairs of shoulder straps, which were manufactured to a variety of designs. Lower ranks had brown straps with silver-grey piping and a system of similarly coloured bars of varying width to indicate seniority, while higher ranks kept the edging but had various combinations of silver-white and gold-yellow thread and other similarly coloured pips. Collar patches worn in pairs provided less information on rank. Up to the level of Generalführer, they consisted of a grey background with silver-white twisted cord edging and a yellow-edged red cross in either the lower left or lower right corner. Above the Generalführer grade, the only embellishment was the replacement of the silver-white cord with gold-yellow edging. Female members of the organisation had a different system of rank identification. On nursing uniforms, different numbers of dark blue pips were embroidered onto the collars.

Personnel also wore a variety of arm badges to denote status and the district to which they belonged. Full-time doctors, both male and female, were often identified by a mid-brown lozenge-shaped badge on which was superimposed in white the traditional medical emblem of a snake twisted around a staff; a similar emblem but with a round green background was also used to indicate qualified volunteers. Both were worn on the lower left sleeve. Female nursing staff also wore a triangular badge on their upper right arm to indicate the administrative district to which they belonged. This consisted of a brown background on which appeared an edging, a version of the eagle and swastika and details of the particular district in Gothic script. All of the latter devices were woven by machine in silver-white thread, although some, possibly privately sourced examples, occur with silver-white hand-embroidered threads.

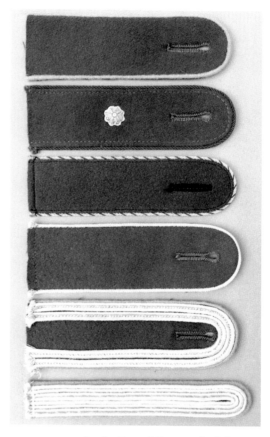

ABOVE: **A selection of German Red Cross (Deutsches Rotes Kreuz) shoulder straps, a mixture of the two known introductions of September 1935 and January 1938. Two of these straps are so far unidentified. Charcoal-grey was the colour chosen for the DRK uniforms and this was the basic colour used for the cloth of the straps worn by lower ranks. Identification from top to bottom: Anwärter and DRK-Helfer; Unidentified but possibly pre-1935 DRK-Vorhelfer; unidentified; repeat strap for a Candidate and German Red Cross Helper; believed to be for a DRK-Oberhelfer; an officer's strap for a DRK-Wachtführer.**

RIGHT: A small group of DRK collar patches of the pattern introduced in 1935. Unlike the cloth of the shoulder straps that matched the material of the charcoal grey German Red Cross uniforms, the cloth used for the collar patches was in a lighter shade of grey. These patches with the red-enamelled Red Cross emblem were worn by both male and female ranks on collars of their service tunics. However, in 1938 the rank insignia for female nurses and leaders underwent a complete change when a different system of rank pips in white metal or dark blue embroidery, depending on the colour of the garment, and in gold pips and small golden oak leaves for senior ranks, was introduced for wear on the collars of their service jackets and work blouses.

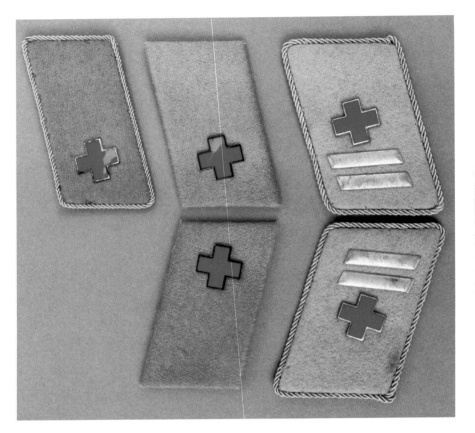

LEFT: A photograph taken on the occasion of the departure of a contingent of French and Walloon volunteers to serve in the Waffen-SS. They are accompanied by Red Cross nursing sisters, all of whom are wearing the DRK duty armband.

OPPOSITE, BELOW: The new 1938 Red Cross uniform regulations introduced arm triangles that were a feature of the uniforms worn by both male and female personnel on the right upper sleeve. These triangles displayed the DRK stylized form of the national emblem set above the name of the wearer's Red Cross location of assignment. Those shown here were of the quality worn by ranks below officer status.

BELOW: The official issue German Red Cross duty armband.

Railway Workers

ABOVE: In September 1941 a series of arm badges were introduced to be worn on the uniform of German railway personnel. They were all yellow on black, machine-woven badges having the German national emblem set above a semicircle of lettering indicating the wearer's railway division or particular function.

Before the war the German railway system was divided into 26 divisions, or Reichsbahndirektionen-RBDs. After the start of the war five additional divisions were created with certain existing RBDs operating the acquired railway systems of Austria, Alsace-Lorraine and Luxemburg. When introduced these arm badges superseded the previous system – a yellow and black arm eagle worn on the left upper arm above a yellow and black cuff-title displaying the name of the wearer's division and function which was worn on the left forearm.

Shown here is a post-1939 badge introduced for those railway workers operating on the Reichsbahndirektion based on Dnepropetrovsk (shown on the badge in its German form as Dnjepropetrowsk) in the Ukraine.

The Nazis reorganised the state railway system as part of their process of transforming the nation's economy and preparing it for war. As part of this Nazification of the system, railway personnel were provided with new uniforms and insignia.

The first major overhaul took place in June 1936, when it was announced that new shoulder straps would henceforth be worn by the railway's 21 separate pay groups but that the collar patches worn previously would remain unaltered. These collar patches, worn in pairs, had separate designs for both open- and closed-neck dark blue tunics and both included a stylised design comprising a single winged wheel on a black background viewed from the side with a red edging. This system remained in place until February 1942, when the old patches were officially abolished and replaced with a new system. These badges again appeared in open- and closed-neck designs and consisted of a black background on which was superimposed various motifs – the organisational symbol, which was reworked to incorporate two wings and the wheel viewed from the front, the swastika, oak leaves, wreaths, and piping.

The shoulder straps introduced in 1936 consisted of various shapes and designs with most having a red edging. Various combinations of bars, pips and piping in gold-yellow and black were used to aid in rank identification. This complex system was supposedly overhauled in September 1941, when a new range of passant shoulder straps was announced with the intention of staggering their introduction over time. The passants, worn in matching pairs, identified individual or groups of ranks/pay grades and all were edged in red. Various other colours, chiefly a darkish blue and gold-yellow, were introduced in various combinations and styles – blocks, plain and chequerboard bars, for example – to differentiate grades.

Railways staff also made use of separate geographical and national arm badges but only for a brief period between February and September 1941. The railway national badge was a variant of the Third Reich emblem – the traditional German eagle holding a wreathed swastika in its talons – and was worn on the upper left sleeve of both the uniform tunic and greatcoat. This insignia was generally worn with a geographical cuff-title of some type. These were worn below the national badge, on the left forearm, and generally comprised a black band edged in yellow with details of wearer's district of service picked out in similarly coloured script. Typically these would consist of 'Reichsbahndirektion' (State Railway Directorate) below which was a zone, usually a major city, such as Berlin, that was a key hub of the national rail network. Variations included the words 'Wehrmacht-Verkehrsdirektion' (Armed Forces Traffic Directorate) with a specific location, such as Paris or Brussels.

These separate arm badges were phased out at the same time in September 1941, when they were united in a single badge worn on the upper left arm of tunics and consisting of a black cloth shield with gold-yellow lettering and insignia. The organisational emblem appeared above lettering that indicated the wearer's directorate (branch of the railway service) and division (area of operations). For example, RVD stood for Reichsverkehrsdirektion (State Traffic Directorate) and HVD for Hauptverkehrsdirektion (Central Traffic Directorate); these were combined with the name of a division either within Germany itself or one of the occupied countries.

Railway staff were also eligible to wear Sparten and Fachabzeichen (branch and specialist badges) on their left forearm. Ten of these were produced and each consisted of a circular black cloth patch on which there was a machine-embroidered design in gold-yellow thread. Some incorporated the organisational emblem or a variation on it, but most consisted of a stylised or representational emblem appropriate to the wearer's position. Carriage supervisors were identified by a side view of a carriage, while machinists wore a cogwheel with lightning bolts, for example.

TOP: **Civilians and railway personnel receiving awards for their conduct during the air raids on Cologne, July 1943.**

ABOVE: **The Ostbahn – Eastern Railways – was the arm badge worn by those railway workers operating in the Eastern Territories and who were not based on any particular railway division.**

LEFT: **The arm badge for the railway division based on Kiev in the Ukraine.**

OPPOSITE, ABOVE: The distinctive green and black armband worn by persons working on the railway system. This band has the ink stamp of the issuing office.

OPPOSITE, BELOW: The short-lived cuff-titles, one for the railway division based on Paris, France, the other for Brussels, Belgium. Shown here for comparison are the two arm badges that replaced these two cuff-titles.

LEFT: The arm badge for the German railway division based on Hanover (note the German spelling of the city – Hannover).

BELOW: Examples of the February 1942 issue of collar patches. Two complete sets of this series of patches were introduced, one for the new open neck tunic and one for the closed neck jackets. The designs displayed on each of these twin sets of patches indicated the wearer's pay grouping, the German Railway workers not actually being classified by ranks.

Postal Services

BELOW: **The German Postal Service had few items of insignia compared with other uniformed civilian organisation. Uniformed postal workers did, however, wear an arm badge, albeit of two versions. The badge shown here was worn by female Post Office personnel on the upper left arm of the new uniforms introduced in 1940.**

A similar badge existed for wear by Post Office personnel who were not qualified as full Post Office functionaries. This version did not display the word 'Deutsche'.

All of Nazi Germany's post, telegraph, and telephone systems, along with some radio stations, were united under the national umbrella organisation known as the **Deutsche Reichspost**. From March 1933 the Reichspost was joined by the **Postschutz** (Postal Protection Service), which was tasked with maintaining the safety and security of all post, telegraph and telephone services throughout the Third Reich. As was common with other state bodies, the identifying insignia and uniforms were modified or created by the Nazi leadership.

Fully qualified members of the Reichspost wore a standard uniform comprising a dark blue jacket and black trousers but embellishments were kept to a minimum. Rank was identified by a range of collar patches, some 20 separate designs in total, that were worn in pairs and edged in orange piping. The eagle and swastika motif was found on various types of headdress. The Reichspost was also aided by numerous auxiliaries, often women and older girls from Nazi youth organisations. Although not entitled to wear a uniform or any systematic insignia, their semi-official status was identifiable by an armband on the upper left arm that comprised a gilt eagle and swastika under which appeared 'Reichspost' in similarly coloured Gothic script. This remained the chief means of identifying such operatives until shortly after the outbreak of World War II. After 1940 they did receive a more formal uniform that consisted of a blue jacket and similarly coloured trousers or skirt. Shirts were left at the discretion of the individual wearer. The uniform was usually accompanied by an eagle and swastika device on the upper left sleeve surrounded by the wording 'Deutsche Reichspost'. Both the lettering and national emblem it surrounded were rendered in gilt and produced on a cloth oval that matched the colour of the tunic.

Members of the Postschutz wore a mid-grey military-style uniform and the organisational badge consisted of the German eagle, which was shown with curved outstretched wings with the head turned to the left from the viewer's perspective, and the usual swastika surrounded by a wreath held in the bird of prey's talons. To indicate the body's connection to the Third Reich's communication's network, two sets of three lightning bolt motifs issued from either side of the upper wreath close to the eagle's talons. The motif was rendered in silver-white thread and placed on a khaki-coloured flattened oval background. The emblem measured 5 cm in height by 8 cm in width. Members of the Postschutz were also identifiable by a cuff-title. Although information is somewhat scanty, some certainly comprised a mid-grey background onto which had been superimposed the word 'Postschutz' in red Gothic lettering. The Postschutz was reorganised in early 1942 and was placed under the direct control of the Reich Ministry of Post and Telegraph and from March came within the orbit of the Allgemeine-SS. Henceforth the body was known as the **SS-Postschutz**. The new body continued to wear its original uniform but the collar insignia were modified to reflect its new links with the SS.

Government Officials

When Hitler came to power in 1933 Germany's administrative services were purged of 'undesirables', chiefly socialists, liberals and Jews, and the remaining bureaucrats underwent a process of Nazification. They had to enroll in the **Reichsbund der Deutschen Beamten** (German Civil Servants' Association), the Nazi Party's union for state functionaries that reached a total membership of 1.2 million, take an oath of allegiance to Hitler, and always use the Nazi salute as a greeting. Civil servants also had to conform to the various other – often petty – obligations placed on them by the new leadership, such as ensuring that their wives conducted themselves in a way befitting state officials and that their children were members of the Hitler Youth, or otherwise face instant dismissal. Nevertheless, the structure and organisation of the various existing departments from the pre-1933 era were left substantially intact, although senior Nazis did take charge of them – Joachim von Ribbentrop, a leading Nazi with little diplomatic experience, took over the Foreign Ministry from Constantin von Neurath, a career diplomat, in 1938, for example – and new ones were created – chiefly the Ministry of Propaganda under Joseph Goebbels and Hermann Goering's Air Ministry – to implement key areas of Nazi policy. As was common throughout the Third Reich, the Nazis introduced a whole range of new insignia to reflect the remoulding of the state bureaucracy and its members.

The organisational emblem chosen for state employees was a variation of the the Nazi state emblem consisting of an eagle holding a wreathed swastika design with both produced in gold-yellow. The range of shoulder straps for government officials to denote seniority was based on the pre-existing system that reflected the bureaucracy's four pay groups, which were simply numbered from one (highest grade) to four. The designs also included a coloured underlay that indicated the wearer's particular branch of service, of which there were four. Those involved in financial, general, internal or special administration had a light grey underlay; officials in the justice department were identified by wine red; the postal section by orange-red; and transport by light red. The various grades of officials in each of these four groupings were indicated by various types of piping placed on the underlay, from simple white to various designs in white and gold-yellow. The Nazi state emblem also appeared across

OPPOSITE, ABOVE: Dr Mastny and wife accompanied by SA-Obergruppenführer Wilhelm Bruckner, Hitler's Chief Adjutant (left) and Reichspräsidialrat Kiewitz (right). Photograph taken in March 1939.

OPPOSITE, BELOW: In a photograph dated 8 December 1942 SS-Obergruppenführer and Reichskommissar for the Occupied Netherlands Reichsminister Dr Seyss-Inquart is shown greeting the Reich Sports Leader von Tschammer und Osten. Seyss-Inquart wears the arm insignia having a horizontal line of four four-pointed stars set inside a large wreath of overlapping oak leaves surmounted by the eagle and swastika. This particular badge with its four stars was worn only by officials with the position of Reichsminister. These and other elaborate sleeve badges indicated the wearer's pay group level. They were not directly connected with rank grades as such.

RIGHT: A prisoner of war exchange under-taken at Barcelona, 27 October 1943. British troops, mostly Australian, recently held in captivity in Germany, about to embark on two British ships, HMSs *Tairia* and *Cuba*, destination the United Kingdom. These ships had brought German exchange prisoners from the Middle East. In the foreground is the German Ambassador to Spain, Dr Hans Heinrich Dieckhoff (in dark greatcoat), seen here during the prelim-inary operations.

BELOW RIGHT: Armband worn by persons in state service.

the centre of the straps in either silver-white or gold-yellow. Groups two to four wore the former, while members of the highest grade carried the latter.

Officials also wore a series of arm badges that were also based on the four-group salary structure and the various designs, with the addition of a varying number of star-shaped pips, to indicate the wearer's grade. Positioned on the lower half of the left sleeve of both the service's formal dark blue dress and grey service uniforms, backgrounds were either black or light grey to blend in with the particular uniform being worn, while there were four distinct designs produced in silver-white. All had the state eagle above horse-shoe shaped motifs of either cording or oak leaves of varying complexity, while the pips denoting rank appeared within both of the former devices.

Eastern Territories Officers

ABOVE: **A Ukrainian Harvest Festival.
A Landwirtschaftsführer (agricultural
farming leader) receiving a gift of a
'harvest crown' from a delegation of
Ukrainian workers.**

itler's plans to create Lebensraum (living space)
for ethnic Germans and support the regime's
economy centred on conquering and then exploiting
the resources of huge swathes of territory in Eastern
Europe. The policy moved into top gear with the
invasion of the Soviet Union in June 1941 and a
month later Alfred Rosenberg, one of Hitler's longest
standing supporters and the Nazi Party's chief
'philosopher', was made head of the
Reichsministerium für die besetzten Ostgebiete
(RMBO/Reich Ministry for the Occupied Eastern
Territories) with its headquarters in Berlin. Rosenberg
headed a vast civil bureaucracy, which was generally
referred to as the Ostministerium (Eastern Ministry).
This oversaw the reorganisation and administration of
the occupied regions, aided in the extermination of
their Jewish communities, and worked with the
Arbeitseinsatzverwaltung (Labour Operations Executive) to provide an
increasingly large pool of slave labour for service in the Third Reich. In June 1944,
for example, Rosenberg ordered the implementation of an operation known as Hau
Aktion (Hay Action), which involved the forcible movement of some 50,000 ten
to fourteen-year-olds from the Eastern Territories to aid the gathering of
Germany's harvest.

RMBO officials operated at various administrative levels in the occupied
territories, from the Reichskommissar responsible for a whole region to the
Gebietskommissar (district commissioner). Beneath the district commissioner
level responsibility for the administration of each Rayon (group of villages) was
left in the hands of local officials or leaders. Four grades of responsibility were
created for members of what was known as the **Führerkorps Ost** (Leadership
Corps East) and each was denoted by designs and colours on collar patches and
cuffs. Four colours were used on collar patches – carmine, dark red, orange and
scarlet red – and these were embellished with various combinations of edging,
piping, pips, oak leaves and the eagle and swastika in silver-white and gold-yellow
to identify either individual or groups of ranks. Reichsminister Rosenberg's
patches consisted of a scarlet red background, which denoted all ministry officials,
edged in gold-yellow superimposed on which were oak leaves and the eagle and
swastika in the same colour.

Members of the Labour Operations Executive wore earth brown uniforms and
rank identification was confined to matching pairs of lozenge-shaped collar
patches which used the same earth-brown colour as the backing for various rank
insignia. The latter included the eagle and swastika, bars, chevrons, pips, edgings,
and oak leaves in various combinations in either silver-white or gold-yellow.
Patches were worn on both uniform tunics and greatcoats.

Ostbau

azi Germany's sweeping military conquests in Eastern Europe between 1939 and 1941 opened up vast territories that were ultimately to be settled by the veterans of Germany's armed forces once the conflict had been successfully concluded. Even before this policy could be enacted, the Lebensraum created in the east at the expense of the original 'racially impure' inhabitants was to be exploited for the benefit of Nazi Germany. However, the conquered lands were notably lacking in the infrastructure – roads and rail networks, for example – that was considered vital to the full use of their natural resources. A body, the Reichs Ministry for the Occupied Eastern Territories, was established under Alfred Rosenberg, to prepare the territories for full-scale Nazi occupation and, as part of this process, the

Ostbau (Eastern Construction) was established to make the region more suitable for German exploitation and settlement. In effect this external organisation paralleled the work undertaken by Nazi Germany's own Reichsarbeitsdienst (State Labour Service), but relied on coercion to accomplish its tasks.

Typical of the organisation was the **Baudienst im Generalgouvernement** (Construction Service in the General Government). The title General Government was given to Nazi-dominated Poland following its conquest in 1939 and the Construction Service was empowered to facilitate the exploitation of the country. Manpower was not a problem as the Nazis simply impressed Poles in their scores of thousands to carry out any work deemed necessary to complete the exploitation programme. These forced workers were treated badly at the very least and at best were provided with only the most basic of 'uniforms' while they toiled under the auspices of the Baudienst.

In contrast, the Baudienst was officered and directed by German personnel and they, at least, received uniforms. Service dress comprised standard items of clothing – trousers, tunics, and so forth – in styles that were commonly found in other branches of the service within the Third Reich. Field grey was commonly used and various emblems and insignia were developed to represent rank, position, and service. Foreign workers from the occupied or nominally liberated lands in the east were also employed in Germany on a voluntary basis in order to alleviate its manpower shortages and the authorities, fearing racial contamination, initially ordered that they had to be identified by a simple badge bearing the word 'Ost' (East) on their outer garments. This caused considerable resentment among those who had chosen to work in Germany on their own initiative and it was abolished in 1944. Devices reflecting the wearer's place of origin were substituted.

ABOVE: **Under the directions of a unit tailor two SS workers are shown how to sew a cuff-band to a tunic. Interestingly the SS style cuff-title displays the lettering 'SS-Baueinsatz-Ost'. As to why it is being positioned directly under the bottom edge of an SS swastika armband the original caption does not say.**

Factory Guards

ABOVE: Almost every factory or place of production throughout the German Reich of any strategic importance employed factory guards as well as its own fire service. For the larger concerns the personnel employed on these duties were frequently distinguished by wearing insignia on their uniforms that displayed the company's emblem. There was a universal arm badge for wear by members of the Factory Protection Service (Werkschutz) consisting of an oval badge of slate-grey cloth having a white rope surround and displaying a Nazi shield protecting a factory building complete with a portion of a cog-wheel. This was worn on the left upper arm. This group of Fire Protection personnel wear uniforms very similar to those worn by the Fire Protection Police. In place of the police arm eagle badge they wear the Werkschutz arm badge, which, in a smaller size and in white metal, is also worn as their cap badge.

The **Werkschutzpolizei** (Factory Protection Police) organisation was created in part to ensure the smooth operation of the Third Reich's economy by protecting important industrial installations and associated infrastructure from disruption either through sabotage or Allied attacks. In the latter case, its work was aided by a parallel organisation known as the **Werkluftschutz** (Factory Air Protection Service). Members of the Factory Protection Police were usually individuals employed privately by a particular business as watchmen or in some similar capacity, but the regulations relating to their terms and conditions of employment came from the Air Ministry and not, as might be expected, from the local police authorities.

The uniforms worn by the Factory Protection Police consisted of the usual range of items – tunics, trousers and so forth – and were of a standard design usually in either a mid-grey or dark blue-black fabric. The arm badge worn on the upper left arm was markedly different from those of most other formations of the Nazi state in that it did not include the traditional German eagle. In contrast it contained several symbols to identify the Factory Protection Police's role within the economy. These included a representation of a factory, complete with chimney, and a stylised cog wheel, all of which were protected by a shield. The badge was worn on the upper left arm of both tunics and greatcoats and comprised an oval background cloth patch in blue-black or mid-grey to match the uniform colour with the various aforementioned designs rendered in silver-white thread. The insignia was completed by a corded edging – also in silver-white – around the central motifs and a black swastika which was superimposed on the shield, The overall badge measured some 7.5 cm in height and 6.5 cm in width. The same factory and shield design was also used as the service's organisational badge and was worn on the peaked cap in a simplified form.

Other identifying insignia included cuff-titles, worn on the lower left arm, which carried the name of the organisation in white lettering on a background to tone in with the uniform colour. Wider armbands were also worn and frequently appeared on the lower left arm with the eagle and swastika emblem. Finally, it was common for individuals responsible for protecting a particular industrial concern to carry some form of identifying emblem on their collar patches that linked them to the particular enterprise. These devices might include a logo or lettering.

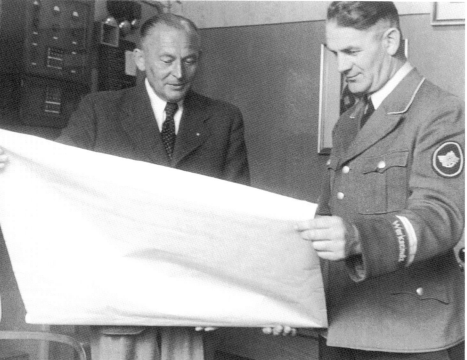

ABOVE: Three members of a factory protection unit conversing amidst the rubble of their place of work. The emblem on the left-hand collar of the man on the right of the picture indicates that his factory was the Junkers Flugzeug- und Motorenwerke AS situated at Dessau in eastern Germany southwest of Berlin and just north of Leipzig.

LEFT: 'These men who are responsible for the security of their factory' . . . so runs the original caption to this photograph. The person on the left is the Werkschutzleiter and the person in uniform is the Oberwachleiter. He wears the cuff-title bearing the legend Werkschutz.

Tram and Bus Officials

BELOW: **The desperate shortage of men, most of whom were serving in the armed forces, meant that tasks such as driving post vans, working for the railway system, driving and conducting trams and omnibuses were tasks easily and skilfully filled by women and girls. Members of the BDM were increasingly employed to act as conductresses on both buses and tramcars. They were distinguished from their company colleagues by wearing armbands that stated they were BDM volunteers. The Berlin 'Bell Fairies' in this photograph wear armbands albeit around the left cuff of their top coats, that state 'BVG Kriegshilfsdienst des Reichsarbeitsdiensten'. Similar armbands were known to have been use, one such having the wording 'BVG Hilfsschaffnerin BDM'.**

Germany had an extensive and efficient public transport system before the Nazis assumed power in 1933, with most settlements larger than small towns having both a bus and tram network. On top of these almost ubiquitous transport services, larger urban areas, such as Berlin, might also have underground systems and be at the hub of motorway and rail routes. The great majority of bus, tram, and underground systems were traditionally owned in whole or part by the local authorities and councils themselves, and the Nazi authorities did not attempt to introduce any sweeping or wide-ranging reforms to the uniforms and insignia worn by their staffs, including the conductresses, who were nicknamed 'Bell Fairies'. Consequently, there was no comprehensive or uniform national dress code or system of rank identification, leaving the provision and style of such items largely in the hands of the local councils.

This is not to say that the Nazis did not impose certain dress and insignia regulations on the local authorities to reflect their assumption of power and the creation of the Third Reich. From 1936 it was made compulsory for all employees to wear the national emblem of Nazi Germany, the eagle and swastika motif, on any headdress, whether side-cap or peaked cap, and certain colours of clothing were expressly forbidden from use. Those colours excluded were associated with the state's armed forces, and included the Army's field grey, the Luftwaffe's blue-grey, and the Nazi Party's own brown, and were commonly known as 'protected uniform colours'. Beyond this the councils were generally allowed to choose any appropriate, usually subdued or neutral hue, for the manufacture of their operatives' dress.

Similarly, for the most part there was no standard national system of rank identification, with decisions once again being taken by the local councils, although the national authorities did make some belated and not wholly successful attempts to regularise the wearing of rank emblems. Aside from indications of rank, which were effectively divided into two groups for those who maintained the buses and trams and those who crewed them, it was common for staff to carry some emblem that reflected their particular company and its location or area of operation. These might comprise armbands or shields worn on the left arm mid-way between elbow and shoulder. Their style and look varied enormously but common motifs included lettering, abbreviations of the company's formal title, or a city's heraldic badge.

Forestry, Hunting and Falconry

The Nazis placed great attachment to the countryside and upheld the traditional rural way of life as both an idyll and an ideal, a cornerstone of the 'true' Germany that was to be preserved and nurtured in the Third Reich. There were three main organisations relating to these aspects of German culture and daily life – the **Deutscher Falkenorden** (German Falconry Order), the **Deutsche Jägerschaft** (German Hunter's Association), of which the Falconry Order was a sub-division, and the State Forestry Service, which was divided into the **Gemeinde Forst Dienst** (General Forestry Service) responsible for state-administered woodlands, and the **Privat Forst Dienst** (Private Forestry Service), which worked with tracts outside the state's immediate control. The Army and Navy also maintained and harvested woodlands under the aegis of their own forestry services and their members wore the same uniform as the state body but with different insignia. The services were organised at the local, district and national level.

Unlike the Forestry Service, both the Falconry Order and Hunting Association dispensed with collar patches to indicate rank and preferred to hand-embroider such details directly onto their uniforms. The insignia were worn in pairs and, in the case of the Falconry Order, which was established in 1938, comprised various numbers of feathers surrounding a stylised falcon. Colours reflected rank, with the head of the service, the Ordenmeister des Deutsches Falkenordens entitled to wear a gold-yellow falcon surrounded by a similarly coloured set of four feathers held together by a looped knot. Hunting Association rank insignia, which underwent several modifications in 1936 and 1938, were initially based on various combinations of oak leaves, pips and wreaths in silver-white or gold-yellow but later included stylised pine branches and deer skulls with antlers. Forestry Service collar patches had a background colour to indicate branch of service (brown in the case of the Private Service) to which various cord edgings and oak leaves were added to indicate rank.

Both hunting and falconry personnel also wore shoulder straps to indicate broad groups of ranks. The overall design was worn by all grades but with the most senior personnel having gold-yellow braiding while others, the majority, employed silver-white braiding. Straps were worn singly between 1934 and 1936 and thereafter worn in pairs. The Forestry Service also used shoulder straps for similar reasons. Among other insignia worn were arm badges. In the case of the Hunting Association and Falconry Order, these included organisational emblems worn on the upper left arm when uniformed that also sometimes appeared in the form of an armband if civilian dress was being worn. Both badges comprised a green flattened oval background with central motifs of an antlered deer skull and hooded falcon respectively. Scrolls, swastikas and sunbursts were also present.

Glossary

Abzeichen
German term for badge.

Aiguilette
A means of identifying rank or status, consisting of variously coloured cords worn over the left or right shoulder by individuals including senior and staff officers, aides, and adjutants, usually as part of the parade uniform.

Alte Kämpfer
Literally meaning 'Old Fighter', a term used to denote a long-standing member of the Nazi Party who had joined before Hitler became chancellor in 1933 and taken part in the early and often violent fight for power that was termed the Kampfzeit ('time of struggle').

Armelstreifen
The German name for the cuff-titles worn for several purposes, such as commemorating an individual or event, the wearer's function, participation in a particular campaign or battle, or unit membership.

BeVo
An acronym trademark developed from the Bandfabrik Ewald Vorsteher enterprise based in Wuppertal that was responsible for producing some of the finest quality silk-woven insignia of the Nazi period.

Bezirksnummer
The identifying number of a particular unit.

Dienstmütze
German word meaning 'service cap', which often referred to a beret-like headdress.

Dienstrock
The basic plain service tunic worn by personnel of the overwhelming majority of Nazi bodies when carrying out their day-to-day activities. They came in a variety of styles and colours but practicality was essential.

Dienststellenabzeichen
Literally meaning 'service position badge',

these were used to indicate the wearer's rank or position within a particular body.

Dress
A catch-all word used to describe a particular style of uniform that was worn on appropriate occasions. Among the types and styles found are Service and Ceremonial appropriate for normal, day-to-day wear or special events respectively.

Fatigues
Term used to describe simple but hard-wearing clothing worn by personnel engaged on difficult, dangerous, or dirty work, such as clearing up debris after an air raid.

Feldbluse
The standard field grey tunic with two breast and two side pockets worn by the German Army from 1935; the simpler Luftwaffe equivalent, which initially dispensed with the breast pockets and had hidden buttons, was known as the Fliegerbluse (flying tunic).

Feldmütze
The standard cloth side cap worn by Army personnel. Similar headgear was worn by other branches of service, such as the Bergmütze (mountain troops) and the Fliegermütze (Air Force personnel).

Fliegerbluse
The flight blouse worn by Air Force personnel. It was a modified version of other tunics that dispensed with long 'skirts', had no cuffs, and often smaller pockets. The aim was to make movement in the confines of an aircraft easier. A similar jacket was also adopted by tank crews.

Gestapo
The Geheime Staatspolizei (State Secret Police) was established by Adolf Hitler to maintain the security of the Third Reich by acting ruthlessly against dissidents and political opponents.

Gorget
A small metal shield worn around the neck and usual held in position by a length of chain. It was most often used to indicate a particular duty and was most commonly, although by no means exclusively, associated with military police officials.

Grey Mice
Name given to members of the Nachrichtenhelferin des Heeres, female auxiliaries operating in the German Army's signals department. The term was coined because the women wore grey uniforms.

Grosser Gesellschaftanzug
Term meaning the full-dress uniform worn for formal occasions.

Hakenkreuz
German for 'hooked cross', the swastika, that became the key symbol for the Nazi Party and, with the traditional national eagle, the Third Reich. The design's origins stretch back to the ancient world – swastika is derived from the Sanskrit for well-being – but in 1910 a German poet, Guido von List, argued that it should be worn by the country's anti-Jewish groups in the erroneous belief that it was Teutonic in origin. It was formally adopted by the Nazis in 1919 and made the central feature of the national flag in 1935.

Helferin
Term meaning female auxiliaries and used to refer to individuals who were attached to a wide range of official organisations but did not enjoy equal status with full time members.

Jahresband
A year band cuff-title that gave details of the wearer's date of membership of a particular organisation.

Kampfbinde
Meaning struggle band, this was the title given to the red, white and black swastika armband adopted by the Nazis in their early days which later became the central and

most ubiquitous icon of the Third Reich.

Landdienst
Land Service was introduced in 1934, with both boys and girls encouraged to serve in the countryside for 12 months.

Lampassen
A double stripe with piping separated by piping that runs down the outer seam of the trousers and was worn by officers to denote their status. In the German Army they were most commonly crimson red.

Litzen
Traditional Prussian collar bars found on collar patches. When seen in pairs they were known as Doppellitzen ('double Litzen').

Ordensburgen
Leadership Schools created by the Nazis to train future members of the party and effective members of the state apparatus. Three were established at Krössinsee, Sonthofen and Vogelsang.

ORPO
An acronym for the *Ordnungspolizei* (Order Police), the Third Reich's major uniformed police force, which was the umbrella organisation that oversaw operations by the Nazi state's various law-enforcement agencies

Passant
A type of narrow shoulder strap decorated with lace or embroidery and worn across or along the shoulder and sometimes used to hold more ornate epaulettes in place.

RADwJ
The Reichsarbeitsdienst der weiblichen Jugend was the Women's (Female Youth) section of the State Labour Service. Initially, the women, who were drawn from the Bund deutscher Mädel, served with the RADwJ for six months but wartime needs meant than many remained for extended periods.

RSHA
The Reichssicherheitshauptamt (Reich Main Security Office) was the central security department of the Nazi government and was created in 1939 to combine the efforts of the various police and security services.

Raute
German term for arm badge.

RMBO
An acronym for the Reichsministerium für die besetzten Ostgebiete (Reich Ministry for the Occupied Eastern Territories), which was established to oversee Nazi activities in conquered lands such as Poland. These included implementing the extermination of their Jewish communities, organising slave labour and preparing the area for German colonisation.

Runic alphabet
An alphabet of 24, later 16, angular characters, probably derived from Greek and Latin, that was used for inscriptions and magic symbols by Germanic peoples, particularly Anglo-Saxons and Scandinavians, between the 3rd and 13th centuries AD. Runes were adopted by the Nazis and used on several badges. One of the most common was known as the Tyr rune. Named after the son of Odin, it comprised an arrow pointing upwards and was often seen on the upper left arm to indicate that the wearer had graduated from the SA's leadership school based in Munich.

Schwalbennester
Literally 'swallows' nests', this term refers to musicians' wings worn on the shoulders, which have a passing resemblance to the mud nests constructed by swallows under the eaves of buildings.

SHD
The Sicherheits und Hilfsdienst (Security and Assistance Service) was part of Germany's response to the Allied strategic bombing offensive and was a conscript force that was responsible for dealing with the aftermath of air raids. Members were exempted from military service but could undertake any other activities while serving with the SHD.

SD
The Sicherheitsdienst (Security Service) was founded in March 1934 as the intelligence-gathering arm of the SS and was headed by Reinhard Heydrich and later Ernst Kaltenbrunner. Its chief role was to ensure the security of Hitler, the Nazi leadership and the stability of the Third Reich. The SD became so powerful that it also oversaw the activities of various other services, including the SIPO and KRIPO (Kriminalpolizei – Criminal Police) and RSHA.

SIPO
An acronym for the Sicherheitspolizei (Security Police), one of two national police forces created by Heinrich Himmler. Its chief components were the Gestapo and the Kriminalpolizei.

Substantive badges
Term given to insignia that are carried by those entitled to a permanent rank by contrast with non-substantive badges that generally denote a trade, skill or proficiency.

Sutterlin
A term denoting the traditional German hand-written script used on some cloth badges. Arabic, Roman, Gothic, copperplate, and Cyrillic scripts were also used in the production of insignia.

Tally
The term for the band of ribbon worn around a naval rating's cap that includes lettering, usually denoting his warship. In the Kriegsmarine the ribbon was usually black and the lettering gold-yellow. In wartime the ship's name was removed for security reasons and replaced with the catch-all title 'Kriegsmarine'.

Verdienstabzeichen
Term meaning length of service or merit badges. For example, cuff-titles with specific dates, varying numbers and thickness of bands on the lower arm and chevrons on the upper arm were all used by the Nazis to indicate prolonged or special service among members of the party.

Waffenfarben
The branch-of-service colours usually found on the edging of shoulder straps and the piping of the Feldmütze. White was used to identify infantry; artillery bright red; mountain troops and Jägers light green; motorised infantry grass green; engineers black; signals lemon yellow; armour salmon pink, and motorised reconnaissance brown.

Wehrmacht
The German armed forces under the Nazis, comprising the Heer (Army), Kriegsmarine (Navy), and Luftwaffe (Air Force). Central control was exercised through the Oberkommando der Wehrmacht (OKW/Armed Forces High Command) although this body's authority was effectively reduced by Hitler's assumption of the role of supreme commander.

Bibliography

The works selected below fall into three main categories and are included to provide a detailed overview of not only Nazi badges and other insignia but also a history of the key period from the end of World War I to 1945. First, there are volumes that look purely at the history, uniforms and insignia of the various military, paramilitary, administrative and civilian units and bodies associated with the Nazis and their regime; second, there are entries that cover Hitler's rise to power during the 1920s and early 1930s, the history of the Nazi Party and the structure of the Third Reich; and third there are background military history and associated reference books dealing with the course of World War II.

Abbott, Peter, Thomas, Nigel, and Chappell, Mike: *Germany's Eastern Front Allies, 1941–45*. Osprey Publishing Limited, London, 1982.

Allen William Sheridan: *The Nazi Seizure of Power*. London and Chicago, 1965.

Andreyev, C.: *Vlasov and the Russian Liberation Movement*. Cambridge, 1987.

Angolia, John: *Cloth Insignia of the SS*. R. James Bender Publishing Co., San Jose, California, 1983

Bender R. J.: *The Luftwaffe*. R. James Bender Publishing Co., San Jose, California, n. d.

Bender, R. J.: *Uniforms, Organisation and History of the Waffen-SS*. (4 vols.) R. James Bender Publishing Co., San Jose, California.

Bender, R. J., and Law R. D.: *Uniforms, Organisation & History of the Afrika Korps*. R. James Bender Publishing Co., San Jose, California, 1974.

Bender, R. J., and Odegard W.: *Panzertruppe – Uniforms, Organisation and History*.
R. James Bender Publishing Co., San Jose, California, 1980.

Bessel, R (ed.): *Life in the Third Reich*. Oxford, 1987.

Bidwell, Brigadier Shelford (consultant editor): *Hitler's Generals and Their Battles – The Men Who Led Germany's Armies to Victory and to Defeat*. Leisure Books, 1984.

Broszat, Martin: *The Hitler State*. Longman, London, 1981.

Bullock, Alan: *Hitler: A Study in Tyranny*. Harper and Row Publishers Incorporated, New York ,1964.

Buss, Michael D., and Mollo, Andrew: H*itler's Germanic Legions*. Macdonald & Jane's Limited, London, 1978.

Cooper, Martin, and Lucas, James: *Panzer – The Armoured Force of the Third Reich*. Macdonald and Jane's Publishers Limited, 1976.

Cooper, Martin: *The German Air Force, 1933–1945: An Anatomy of Failure*. London, 1981.

Dallin, Alexander: *German Rule in Russia, 1941-1945*. London and New York, 1957.

Davis, Brian Leigh: *German Parachute Forces, 1935–45*. Arms and Armour Press, London, n. d.

Davis, Brian Leigh: *German Uniforms of the Third Reich, 1933–45*. Blandford Press, Poole.

Davis, Brian Leigh: *German Army Uniforms and Insignia, 1933–45*. Arms and Armour Press, London, 1971

Davis, Brian Leigh: *Badges and Insignia of the Third Reich, 1933–1945*. Blandford Press, Poole, 1983.

Davis, Brian Leigh: *Uniforms and Insignia of the Luftwaffe*, 1933–1945 (2 vols.). Blandford Press, Poole.

Davis, Brian Leigh: *Flags of the Third Reich (1) – Wehrmacht*. Osprey Publishing Limited, London, 1994.

Davis, Brian Leigh: *Flags of the Third Reich (3) – Party and Police Units*. Osprey Publishing Limited, London, 1994

Davis, W. J. K., *German Army Handbook*. Ian Allan Ltd, 1973.

Dear, I. C. B. (General Editor): *The Oxford Companion to World War II*. Oxford University Press, 2001.

Dupuy, Trevor N., Johnson, Curt, and Bongard, David L.: *The Harper Encyclopedia of Military Biography*. HarperCollins Publishers, Inc., New York, 1992.

Ellis, Chris: *A Collector's Guide to the History and Uniforms of Das Heer – The German Army 1937–45*. Ian Allan Publishing, 1993

Ellis, Chris: *21st Panzer Division – Rommel's Afrika Korps Spearhead*. Ian Allan Publishing, 2001.

Fest, Joachim C.: *The Face of the Third Reich*. New York and London, 1972.

Fest, Joachim C.: *Hitler*. Weidenfeld & Nicolson, London, 1974.

Freeman, M: *Atlas of Nazi Germany*. New York, 1987.

Gilbert, Martin: *The Final Journey – The Fate of the Jews in Nazi Europe*. Allen & Unwin, London, 1979.

Gordon-Douglas, S. R.: *German Combat Uniforms, 1939–1945*. Almark, 1970.

Grünberger, Richard: *A Social History of the Third Reich*. Weidenfeld & Nicolson, London, 1971.

Höhne, Heinz: *The Order of the Death's Head – The History of the SS*. Secker & Warburg, London, 1969.

Humble, Richard: *Hitler's High Seas Fleet*. Ballantine Books, London, 1971.

Jurado, Carlos Caballero: *Foreign Volunteers of the Wehrmacht, 1941–45*. Osprey Publishing Limited, London, 1983.

Jurado, Carlos Caballero: *The German Freikorps, 1918–23*. Osprey Publishing Limited, London, 2001

Jurado, Carlos Caballero, and Thomas, Nigel: *Germany's Eastern Front Allies (2) – Baltic Forces*. Osprey Publishing Limited, London, 2002.

Keegan, John: *Waffen SS – The Asphalt Soldiers*. Ballantine Books, New York, 1970.

Keegan, J. (ed): *Who's Who in World War II*. Routledge, London, 1995.

Krawczyk, Wade, and Lukacs, Peter V., *Waffen-SS Uniforms and Insignia*. The Crowood Press, 2001.

Leach, B.: *German Strategy in Russia*. Oxford University Press, London and New York, 1973

Littlejohn, David: *The SA, 1921–45 – Hitler's Stormtroopers*. Osprey Publishing Limited, London, 1990.

Lucas, James: *War on the Eastern Front – The German Soldier in Russia, 1941–45*. Jane's Publishing Company, 1979.

Lucas, James: *Storming Eagles – German Airborne Forces in World War Two*. Arms and Armour Press, London, 1988.

Lumsden, Robin: *The Allgemeine-SS*. Osprey Publishing Limited, London, 1993.

Lumsden, Robin: *SS Regalia*. Bison Books Limited, London, 1995

Lumsden, Robin: *Collector's Guide to Third Reich Militaria*. Ian Allan Publishing Limited.

Lumsden, Robin: *Collector's Guide to the Waffen-SS*. Ian Allan Publishing Limited.

Lumsden, Robin: *Collector's Guide to the Allgemeine-SS*. Ian Allan Publishing Limited, 2002.

Macksey, Major K. J.: *Panzer Division – The Mailed Fist*. Macdonald and Co., London, 1968.

Mallmann Showell, J. P. : *The German Navy in World War II*. London, 1979.

Mason, David: *U-boat – The Secret Menace*. Ballantine Books Ltd., London, 1972.

Mollo, Andrew: *Army Uniforms of World War II*. Blandford Press, Poole, n. d.

Mollo, Andrew: *German Uniforms of World War 2*. Macdonald & Jane's.

Mollo, Andrew: *Uniforms of the SS*: (7 vols.): Historical Research Unit, London, 1969–76.

Mollo, Andrew: *The Armed Forces of World War II – Uniforms, Insignia and Organisation*. Orbis Publishing, London, 1981.

O'Neill, Robert J.: *The German Army and the Nazi Party, 1933–1939*. Cassell and Co. Limited, London, 1966.

Orlow, Dietrich: *The History of the Nazi Party, 1919–1933*. Pittsburgh, 1969

Overy, R. J.: *The Penguin Historical Dictionary of the Third Reich*. Penguin Books, London, 1996.

Pia, J.: *SS Regalia*. Ballantine Books Limited, New York, 1974.

Quarrie, Bruce: *Afrika Korps*. Patrick Stephens Limited, Cambridge, 1975.

Quarrie, Bruce: *World War II Photo Album Number 1 – Panzers in the Desert*. Patrick Stevens Limited, Cambridge, 1978.

Quarrie, Bruce: *Waffen-SS Soldier, 1940–45*. Osprey Publishing Limited, London, 1993

Quarrie, Bruce: *7th Flieger Division: Student's Fallschirmjäger Elite*. Ian Allan Publishing, 2001.

Reitlinger, Gerald: *SS– Alibi of a Nation*. William Heinemann Limited, London, 1957.

Rempel, G., *Hitler's Children*. Chapel Hill, North Carolina, 1989.

Rosignoli, Guido: *Army Badges and Insignia of World War 2* (2 vols.). Blandford Press, Poole.

Ruffner, Kevin Conley: *Luftwaffe Field Divisions, 1941–45*. Osprey Publishing Limited, London, 1990.

Schoenbaum, David: *Hitler's Social Revolution*. Weidenfeld and Nicolson, London, 1967.

Scurr, John: *Germany's Spanish Volunteers, 1941–45*. Osprey Publishing Limited, London, 1980.

Sharpe, Michael, and Davis Brian L.: *Grossdeutschland – Guderian's Eastern Front Elite*. Ian Allan Publishing, 2001.

Shirer, William L.: *A Berlin Diary*. New York and London, 1941

Shirer, William L. *The Rise and Fall of the Third Reich*. Secker & Warburg, London, 1960.

Shores, Christopher: *Spanish Civil War Air Forces*. Osprey Publishing Ltd, London, 1977

Smelser, R.: *Robert Ley – Hitler's Labour Front Leader*. Oxford, 1988.

Snyder, Dr. Louis L.: *Encyclopedia of the Third Reich*. McGraw Hill, Incorporated, 1976.

Speer, Albert: *Inside the Third Reich*. Macmillan, London, 1970.

Stein, G. H., *The Waffen SS: Hitler's Elite Guard at War, 1939–1945*. London, 1966.

Stern, J. P.: *The Führer and the People*. Berkeley, California, 1975.

Seydewitz, Max: *Civil Life in Wartime Germany*. Viking Press, New York, 1945.

Taylor, A. J. P.: *The Origins of the Second World War*. Hamish Hamilton, Macmillan, London, 1961.

Taylor, James, and Shaw, Warren: *Dictionary of the Third Reich*. Penguin Books, London, 1997.

Thomas, Nigel: *The German Army, 1939–45 (1) – Blitzkrieg*. Osprey Publishing Limited, London, 1997.

Thomas, Nigel: *The German Army, 1939–45 (2) – North Afrika & Balkans*. Osprey Publishing Limited, London, 1998.

Thomas, Nigel: *The German Army 1939–45 (5) – Western Front, 1943–45*. Osprey Publishing Limited, London, 2000.

Toland, John: *Adolf Hitler*. Random House, New York, 1976.

Trevor-Roper, Hugh R.: *The Last Days of Hitler*. MacMillan, London, 1962.

Tusa Ann, and Tusa, John: *The Nuremberg Trial*, Macmillan, London. 1983.

Ulric of England: *SS and Political Cuffbands*. Ulric Publishing, Surrey, 1998.

Wheal, Elizabeth-Anne, and Pope, Steven: *The Macmillan Dictionary of the Second World War*. Macmillan, London, 1997.

Williamson, Gordon: *German Military Police Units, 1939–45*. Osprey Publishing Limited, London, 1989.

Williamson, Gordon: *Afrikakorps, 1941–1943*. Osprey Publishing Limited, London, 1991.

Williamson, Gordon: *German Mountain & Ski Troops, 1939–45*. Osprey Publishing Limited, London, 1996.

Williamson, Gordon: *German Seaman, 1939–45*. Osprey Publishing Limited, London, 2001.

Williamson, Gordon: *German Battle Insignia*. Osprey Publishing Limited, London, 2002.

Windrow, Martin: *World War 2 Combat Uniforms and Insignia*. Patrick Stevens Limited, 1977.

Windrow, Martin: *The Panzer Division*. Osprey Publishing Limited, London, 1982.

Windrow, Martin: *The Waffen-SS*. Osprey Publishing Limited, London, 1982

Young, Brigadier Peter (editor). *The World Almanac of World War II*, Bison Books Ltd, London, 1981.

Index